A New Approach to Industrial Economics

Other Books by James F. Lincoln

LINCOLN'S INCENTIVE SYSTEM
INCENTIVE MANAGEMENT

James F. Lincoln

Chairman of the Board
The Lincoln Electric Company, Cleveland, Ohio

A New Approach to Industrial Economics

The Devin-Adair Company
New York, 1961

First Printing—1961

Reprinted by
The Lincoln Electric Company
through special arrangement with
the original publisher,
The Devin-Adair Company

Printed in U. S. A.

Preface

Industry in America is facing a crisis. The program used by industrial leadership is not succeeding under the new conditions that have developed. Technical development has shrunk the world to a small part of what it was only a few years ago. This development has had a great effect on all people in many ways. Its effect is greatest in industry, with its present widely varying wage rates and widely different customs in different countries and its different worker-management relations. The industrial problem therefore is greatly changed from what it was. And it is becoming more involved in America, as the competition from abroad that has been induced by these changes, increases.

The methods, machinery and needs of the situation must now be reviewed, since we are being outdistanced by foreign competition. New programs must be developed if we are to keep our place in the family of nations.

Some producers recommend the application of protective tariffs to eliminate foreign competition as an answer to the problem. Reducing the power of the unions is also suggested. If we will only be objective in our thinking we shall see that such actions could never do more than give at best temporary relief. That is not the real answer. America has met such problems before. We must meet them now, head on.

The program outlined in this text is an answer that is fundamentally sound, since it is based on a sound philosophy. It has proven itself by long experience. It cannot fail, if used. Its handicap is that it is contrary to present custom. It is obvious that any plan that will succeed must be contrary to present custom, since present custom has failed. A successful solution, therefore, would have to be different.

JAMES F. LINCOLN

Cleveland, Ohio
July, 1961

Contents

Acknowledgment

I want to express my thanks to Miss Marjorie Wilkie, who did the copy work on the manuscript, and to Mrs. Rose Wilder Lane, who has been very helpful with suggestions. The philosophy and example of Dr. Frank Halliday Ferris have been fundamental in developing this approach. I am very grateful to him.

JAMES F. LINCOLN

Prologue

James Finney Lincoln: A Profile

I F a man were known only "by the company he keeps," James Finney Lincoln would be a hard man "to know." He is not a gregarious person. Outside of his pastor and perhaps a few people in the educational world his friendships have been casual. These biographical notes are added here to contribute hopefully, to a fuller appreciation of what James Lincoln has done and said.

The Lincoln heritage is one of strength and other qualities, reaching back to the early years of our country and to England. James Lincoln would be no stranger in a gathering of his ancestors.

His father, William Elleby Lincoln, was a minister

of the Gospel, a fervent abolitionist, firm in his convictions, strong minded, strong willed and articulating his convictions without reservation in both his preaching and his actions. James' paternal great-grandfather named John Cromwell was a pioneering surgeon in London. His grandfather was also a physician. His mother, Louisa Marshall, was an educated woman who traced her family lineage in this country to 1634. One of their great interests was education. They became influential in their times through careers in journalism and publishing.

William Elleby Lincoln came to America in 1853 as a young man in his early twenties inspired by the preaching of Charles Grandison Finney, in whose honor and memory James was given his middle name. Finney was then President of Oberlin College, Ohio and pastor of the First Congregational Church at Oberlin. He was preaching in England and fired the young William with his zeal. Finney was a famous revivalist, strongly anti-slavery and anti-mason. William made his way to Oberlin and entered the college there to prepare for a life of preaching. He was close to the college, its intellectual and moral atmosphere, for the next ten years, from which he derived the direction and drive for his life's energies. The Oberlin atmosphere was strongly religious, stressed individualism, both of which morally were to be expressed in efforts towards social reform. Slavery was one of the chief targets at that time.

It was here that he met Louisa Marshall, a tall woman of strong character. Impulsively, William pro-

posed marriage before he had finished seminary which
was against the established rules. She accepted, ap-
parently sharing his strong convictions and dedication
to a life of service, perhaps also feeling that she could
serve as a balance wheel in what promised to be a
stormy career. They were married and as a consequence,
he did not receive his degree from the seminary. He
was, however, later ordained in the Congregational
Church and after a brief period of teaching at Berea
College in Kentucky, he turned to the pastorate and a
life of preaching which did indeed prove to be stormy.
The controversial nature of some of his ideas, and his
unhesitating expression of them frequently were the
cause of a change in congregations which he served.
Through this "itinerate pastorate" Louisa did serve as a
balance and her kind and friendly nature made a home
for their children whom she also reared in the demands
of her faith.

After almost 18 years of "wandering," the family
eventually settled in Painesville, Ohio on the farm of
Louisa Marshall's parents. Here, James Finney Lincoln
was born on May 14, 1883. He had two older brothers
and a sister. With his father still devoted to preaching, his mother's time full with the family duties and
her other interests, and his brothers at school, the
work of the farm naturally fell to James at an early
age. Fortunately, he was well endowed physically, and
the farm and family chores found broad shoulders on
which to fall. The word lazy he did not understand. He
drove himself at his tasks with his inherited ability to

3

concentrate his efforts on the job to be done. He walked
7 miles a day to school in Painesville.

His evenings were spent studying and listening to his
father read aloud from the Bible. The Sermon on the
Mount became as well known to him as the multiplication table and American History. He learned to pray.
He learned to think with simple logic. He had many
hours alone, working and going to and from school, to
begin to formulate his ideas that were later to form
his philosophy as a man of industry—not as a blacksmith which had been his boyhood ambition. From the
straightforward announcements in the Sermon on the
Mount he learned God's laws of life, principal among
which is that life is not a solo performance but must be
played out together in family, society, and business. His
ambition to be a blacksmith proves he had come to see
the dignity of hard labor and the justice of being rewarded in direct proportion to effort and ability.

James' development in these years of his youth was
influenced much by his mother. Her kindly and friendly
nature tempered the "climate" of the home. Her interest
in education served as an inspiration. Her life was an
example of stewardship—the development of her God-
given talents to their fullest and their devotion to useful
purposes.

Following the heritage of his family and the example
of his two older brothers, James began to prepare himself physically, mentally, and financially to go to the
Ohio State University. By the time he was 20, he had
saved enough money, which, with a timely loan from

4

his older brother who had finished at Ohio State, enabled him to take up his study of electrical engineering at Columbus.

Although his scholastic career was little more than average, James' athletic career was a considerable cut above the average. His 6' 2" and 202 pound frame quickly qualified him for the football team. He played all four years of his college life and captained the team in his senior year. He was and is one of Ohio State's outstanding fullbacks. During his captaincy, the Ohio State goal line was never crossed. He played every minute of 10 games. His football experiences made a deep impression on his character—it gave expression to his tremendous physical drive. He learned to take hurts and defeats yet get up again and keep driving. He realized that it is only the entire team effort that gets the ball across the goal line. Perhaps the most important thing he learned was the incentive of recognition for achievement.

While young Jim was growing up and going to school, his oldest brother John, 17 years his senior, had entered the young electrical industry. He worked for several companies, among them Brush Electric. He then decided to start his own company. In 1895 the Lincoln Electric Company began repairing and making electric motors in the basement of John's home, on $150 of borrowed capital. The young company had a hard struggle, and the college student Lincoln was a welcome addition to the work force during his summer vacations. He learned the practical side of electrical engineering that

5

he was studying and had an opportunity to see the problems of operating and managing a small shop.

In the spring of 1907 James fell sick with typhoid fever and was forced to drop out of school. When he recovered he was faced with a difficult decision. He knew he had a job waiting for him. He did not graduate. With characteristic decisiveness he went to work without the sheepskin, the achievement of which he felt would add little to his knowledge of electrical engineering. He went on the Lincoln Electric Company payroll April 1st, 1907, as the company's only salesman, working for $50 a month plus 2% sales commission.

By the time James joined his brother John, the young Lincoln Electric Company had gone through its birth pains and early youth. The company was established in the electric motor business and just moving into a new building which it had constructed. John, however, was more interested in exercising his engineering genius than his business abilities. He made an electrical automobile drive with a regenerative brake. He also began to develop techniques for bonding electrical connections on the rails of electric railways. When he had been with Brush he had worked on developing the new carbon arc light and therefore was familiar with arc phenomena. He put the carbon arc to work making rail bonds.

It was into this period that James was cast as a salesman. The situation was almost made to his order and he immediately put to work his energy, drive and dedication to purpose. He soon saw the necessity of concentrating the efforts and interests of the company. The diversification of engineering talents and manufacturing efforts were sapping the profits of the company which desperately needed growth capital to realize the potential of the ideas it was creating.

John recognized his younger brother's business talents as contrasted with his own engineering interests and quickly assigned responsibilities on which these talents could be exercised. James was made Vice President of the Company in 1911. Three years later in 1914, with the crisis of World War I facing the company, he was made General Manager. He was 31 years old. His brother John was 48. The younger man moved quickly into the situation, applying a firm hand to rectify the company's shaky financial situation and somewhat erratic business policies.

One of the first actions he took as General Manager might appear to be somewhat out of character for a man of his nature and background, but actually it was not. Rather it proved to be a most characteristic action in the light of the subsequent history of his management ideas. Realizing that he was relatively young and inexperienced, yet desiring desperately to succeed in business and personally, he called together the people of the company and asked them to elect representatives from each department who would sit with him and advise him on the company's operations. The group was to be purely advisory in function, but was to have no limits on the scope of its interests and concerns. Mr. Lincoln in writing later about this group said, "I knew

7

that if I could get the people in the company to want the company to succeed as badly as I did, there would be no problems we could not solve together." Thus was started the Advisory Board of the Lincoln Electric Company which has met twice a month every month since 1914, and from whose counsels and suggestions have come many of the people and ideas with which the company was to grow to its present stature.

The company had made a few welding machines, beginning in 1907, using the general design and materials incorporated in the company's motor-generator, battery charging machines. The war brought an abrupt end to the electrical automobile and consequently the battery charger business. The war also brought to a dramatic spotlight, the potentials of arc welding. Times provided the opportunity. Lincoln provided the vision. He saw arc welding as much more than a repair tool. He could see it as the logical and best way to join any two metals together not only for repair purpose, but also for factory production of machinery and equipment and in construction work of all types. He set for his company the goal of making this rather specialized electrical phenomenon a commercially practical and useful process. Without disregarding the company's staple motor business which flourished well during the war, he turned the creative energy of the organization to arc welding.

Typical of both his foresight and determination, was a trip he made to Washington, D. C., during the early days of the war, to visit a top Admiral in the Navy. His purpose was to convince the Navy that they could build lighter, stronger and faster ships with welding than they could with riveting. The Admiral, perhaps visualizing welding as some sort of "gluing" technique, concluded the interview with the rather rash comment that he would kick off with his toe any weld Mr. Lincoln could make. It wasn't until 1938 that the German Navy, limited by the Versaille Treaty, proved Mr. Lincoln right by turning to welding so they could mount heavier armament on lighter ships and remain within the treaty limits. Thus Lincoln very early saw the need to educate and train people in the use of welding. The company started a welding school in 1917 and has operated it continuously ever since.

The company passed through its adolescent years at the accelerated rate of war times, but came out of the war years firmly established and eager to rise with the industrial boom that was to follow. The company made the most of its opportunities. First it applied welding to its own motor line. Where it had used castings it turned to steel weldments. The weight and cost reduction permitted a price reduction of some 50%. Welded steel construction was applied to the construction of welding machines, with similar success. Mr. Lincoln also went to the Austin Company, engineers and builders, and persuaded them to attempt the construction of a welded building. This first welded building was not exactly a "low cost" structure, but it did mark the beginning of commercial structural welding.

The success of these first applications of welding to commercial production and construction confirmed

9

Lincoln's vision of its potential. He launched an intensive effort to educate engineers and business men to these facts, realizing, of course, that the company would not sell any welding equipment until people decided to use welding in place of other existing methods. The company began to sponsor competitions for design, publish books, conduct seminars, write for technical journals, work with engineering colleges, and even spend its advertising budget for this purpose. In 1936, he established a foundation devoted to the development of arc welding. Lincoln's purpose in all this was to give engineers the information with which they could make an intelligent decision in the light of new developments that they might not otherwise be familiar with.

New ideas in the area of business management also found ready acceptance in the minds of the people who comprised this young, dynamic company. In 1915 each employee was given a paid life insurance policy. In 1919, the employees organized an association for health benefits and social activities. By 1923, employees were given two weeks paid vacations, the shop was operating with a piecework plan, and all earnings were adjusted automatically up or down according to the fluctuations of the cost of living index of the Bureau of Labor. Nineteen hundred twenty-three also saw the company move into a larger plant. In 1925, the Board of Directors voted to make stock available to employees and started a stock purchase plan. In 1929, the Board devised a Suggestion System.

All of these ideas were successful and have been carried on continuously since their inception. All of them were initiated for only one reason—simply because they appeared to be the right thing to do under the circumstances. They were not efforts to buy good behavior. They were not efforts to increase profits. They were not antidotes to labor difficulties. They did not constitute a "do-gooder" program. They were expressions of mutual respect for each person's importance to the job to be done. All of them reflect the leadership of James Lincoln under whom they were nurtured and propagated. He became President of the company in 1928.

The Lincoln Electric Company came through the decade of the 20's a well seasoned team with strong leadership and flexing its muscles for the competitive struggles taking shape in industry. On the eve of the Great Depression it had just introduced a new concept in welding electrodes and developed a new technique for making them that resulted in price reductions of over 50%. The company was promptly sued for patent infringement by one of the industrial giants who considered welding a specialized process that it wanted to control through licensing. James fought back with his usual vigor and won the case, opening the industry for free competition and assuring a future of steadily decreasing costs rather than monopolistic high price levels. Had this not been the outcome, the development of welding would have been significantly retarded, especially with the effect of the Depression compounding the normal deterrent of controlled prices. This was not to be the last time Lincoln found it necessary to champion what he thought to be right, both in and out of the courts of law.

The company had the usual difficulties experienced by manufacturing organizations during the lean years of the Depression. Hours and pay were short. Sales were hard to come by. But the company had one all-important advantage over its contemporaries. Mr. Lincoln by his actions and words through the years since 1914 had given his associates to know that he was completely honest, that he respected their abilities and wanted their cooperation. Problems of the times were thus approached with the idea that together a solution could be found. One of the most significant mutual efforts to arrive at a solution occurred in 1934.

Through the Advisory Board, the employees asked if hours could be increased. This was accepted and in addition a bonus plan was installed. At the end of the year, because of the greater efficiency, the company distributed a cash "bonus" consisting of what money remained after taxes and dividends had been paid. Each person received a bonus which on the average amounted to approximately 30% of what he had earned during the year.

This was the beginning of Lincoln's bonus plan. It has been paid every year since 1934. Through this bonus, Lincoln workers have received over $100 million in addition to the regular earnings which are average for the industry. Thus each person shares in the results of the organization's efficiency and shares according to what he or she has contributed to that efficiency.

12

From this point on, the evolution of Lincoln's ideas was accelerated by the heightened response from Lincoln workers to the need for cooperative efforts. As problems arose, an honest effort was made by all to arrive at the answer which would be best for the company in the long run towards its objective of providing better products at continually lower prices. These ideas followed during the next ten years after the first payment of the year-end bonus: a pension plan for all employees paid for by the company, a job evaluation program for determining base pay rates, a merit rating system for determining each person's share of the year-end bonus, a policy of promotion from within and guaranteed employment.

A company combining a management guided by ideas like these, with a group of people wanting the program to be a success, both engaged in a rapidly expanding industry was inevitably headed for the top. Before the outbreak of World War II the company had become the world's largest manufacturer of arc welding equipment with subsidiary plants in Canada, England and Australia, and licensed manufacture of its products in Brazil, Argentina, and Mexico.

But leadership has its price as well as its rewards. The company's outstanding achievements invited the scrutiny of envy and the criticism of skeptics. Wartime controls on prices and wages led several bureaucratic investigators to examine the operations and unfortunately make superficial evaluations. Lincoln found himself again in the position of having to defend what

13

he knew to be right—as right as the Sermon on the Mount.

The Government sued the company for taxes to which it felt entitled because the company was said to be paying too much money to its workers. The specific arguments were over certain payments the company had made in the years 1940 and 1941, but all of the arguments came down to the point that the company had to prove it was getting a performance from the organization commensurate with its high rate of pay. Lincoln charged into the fight like the fullback he had been, proving beyond question that his program of incentive management was getting results that seemed, at first glance, incredible when compared with the normal performance of industry. The Internal Revenue lawyers dragged the case up and down the courts with appeals, but finally after ten years of litigation Lincoln was vindicated.

Lincoln also crossed swords with the Government over the question of renegotiation of profits made on war business. Lincoln did not question the Government's right to renegotiate but did strongly object to the manner in which the amounts were determined. He countered the Government's claims with his own that his program of incentive management and its effect in reducing prices had saved the Government over $60,-000,000 on welding equipment and supplies used in the war effort. This was true, the Government acknowledged, and then asked him to build a new factory, at Government expense, to increase the production of

14

welding electrodes. Lincoln said no, it would not be necessary. He offered, instead, to go to his competitors and show them how to increase their output by using Lincoln's production techniques, which he did.

The story of welding in World War II was considerably different than it was in World War I. Welding had become accepted as a standard metal joining method in all types of metal working industry. Its economy and inherent advantages of greater strength and rigidity with less material had won it a solid place in manufacturing and construction. The war necessities of speed and making available materials go as far as possible accelerated the use of welding. President Roosevelt acknowledged its vital importance in saying the Liberty Fleet would have been an impossibility without it. The Lincoln Electric Company grew in proportion to the growth in the use of welding. Three shifts a day turned materials out of the Lincoln plant in unprecedented quantities.

The real test of Lincoln's ideas came when they faced the temptations of prosperity. Prosperity tends to make a hard, lean organization somewhat flabby. Prosperity tempts one to charge too much. Prosperity tends to make one profit conscious rather than customer conscious.

However, Lincoln held a steady course. The ideas that had matured in the years of depression and war, came into full flower following World War II. While costs continued to spiral upward, and inflation added its toll, Lincoln kept the objectives of his company clearly set out and declared a goal of reducing its labor and other costs 10% every year. As a result, the prices of welding equipment stayed practically level while the prices of nearly everything going into the products doubled, tripled, and even quadrupled. The company prospered. The welding industry continued to grow.

In 1951 a new 30 acre plant was designed and built in order to be able to incorporate into the very structure itself everything possible to facilitate Lincoln's unique production ideas.

In 1954, Lincoln moved up from President to Chairman of the Board. William Irrgang, a brilliant engineer who had come to this country from Germany and joined the company in 1928 was made President.

The continued progress of the company through the 16 years following World War II in the direction given it by Lincoln's philosophy of incentive management clearly removes any question of validity and refutes the proposition that such efforts require special conditions for success. The fact that similar programs have been equally successful in Lincoln's subsidiary plants should remove any final questioning that the ideas require a special type of person for their execution.

The story of James F. Lincoln is to a large extent the story of the Lincoln Electric Company. His life has been centered in the company and the company is an honest reflection of the man. This brief biography would not be complete, however, without some comment on his personality.

Lincoln has been a man of physical vigor all of his life. In his seventies, his actions are those of a man in his fifties. His blunt drive is expressed in direct action. He is a man of independence, intelligence and courage; completely honest and fair, yet toughminded and uncompromising. He has the zeal of a missionary about almost everything he does. He approaches everything he does, however, with the logic of an engineer. He has been condemned by some business men as a business radical and reformer; yet praised by others as one of the country's outstanding business leaders, a prime example of the nation's disappearing breed of "rugged individualists."

It is not difficult to see how diametrically opposite views regarding the man can be held. He has always spoken out for whatever he believed to be right, both volubly and articulately. He has addressed literally thousands of groups in English speaking countries throughout the world. He is a "constant" contributor to the letters-to-the-editor columns of Cleveland papers. He has written three books. In all of this he has never hesitated to declare his hand, regardless of how the chips might fall.

Collective bargaining he has characterized as "civil war." In 1945, when the Government organized a labor conference to study post war labor-management problems, he sent a telegram to the opening meeting forecasting its failure in saying the conference was simply "writing new rules for continuous war between labor and management instead of seeking to eliminate that war." He has criticized the labor union movement for "selfishly attempting to better its position at the expense of the people it must serve." The growth of Federal Government has been a constant target in his efforts to keep alive the nation's heritage of individualism. He has criticized the Government's programs saying that "coddling drones has probably caused more businesses to go to seed than any other one thing."

When called to Washington to justify his profits in connection with renegotiation of war contracts he took the offensive. "Renegotiation," he said, "penalizes industrial efficiency and if you kill efficiency you could lose the war. If you penalize a man for doing a good job he is not going to do it."

Three days later, the company was offered an Army-Navy "E" pennant. His reaction was fast. "I was dragged to Washington on an investigation and there they told us we were very bad people. When I got back to Cleveland about three days later, they said we were very good people and offered us a pennant. I told them to take their pennant and give it to one of the boys who were good all of the time."

When taken to court over taxes due because he "was paying his people too much" he asked if he would be sued if he had twice as many people on the payroll doing the same amount of work and therefore receiving half as much pay. The answer was no, he would not be sued. His comment was, "The only crime for which we are being fined this way, $1,600,000, is that we have released 2500 men for jobs elsewhere in the war effort."

James Lincoln's life has been shaped largely by his devotion to the company that bears his name. His family he has kept almost as a separate compartment of his life, cherished but demanding a different devotion than his company, and whose independence he has carefully protected. He was married in Cleveland in 1908 to Alice, daughter of David H. Patterson, a manufacturer of that city. They had four children, three daughters and a son, and 21 grandchildren. His wife died in 1954. He married Jane White in 1961. Miss White was Dean of Women of Lake Erie College in Painesville, of which Lincoln has been Chairman of the Board of Trustees for a number of years.

He also has been active in his support of other educational institutions. He has been Chairman of the Board of Trustees of the Ohio State University and President of its Alumni Association, a member of the Board of Trustees of Case Institute of Technology and Fenn College Corporation. His engineering affiliations include the American Society of Electrical Engineers and the American Society of Mechanical Engineers, the American Welding Society, and Cleveland Engineering Society. He had served his industry as President of the National Electrical Manufacturers Association. He is a member of National Industrial Conference Board, National Association of Manufacturers and several Government committees. He has served his commu-

19

nity through church, civic and welfare agencies. He has received several honorary degrees: a D.Sc. from the Ohio State University, LL.D. from Lake Erie College and Oberlin College, and a L.H.D. from Fenn College.

CHARLES G. HERBRUCK

Cleveland, Ohio

A New Approach to Industrial Economics

1

The Economic Problem

N O O N E can view the abuses that are common in our economy without concluding that there are other approaches to our problems, which, if taken, would give far better results.

The philosophy expressed by Christ in his Sermon on the Mount gives the answer that could not fail if we would only accept and follow it in our daily operations. This ethic should be accepted as the guide for our actions, instead of thinking of such a program as a topic for discussion on Sunday and one that has no application during the rest of the week. The Sermon on the Mount is a successful rule of life which man, if he is to remain on earth, eventually must follow. No other program has yet appeared that will better guide man to success and happiness. It is doubtful if man can continue to live as our power of destruction increases, unless he follows the philosophy that Christ announced.

This Christian ethic would give to all a much higher standard of living. It would eliminate the threat of war. It would stop the abuses that because of habit we now accept as normal. It would also make the trend of our economy head toward unimagined greater progress.

The program that Christ announced, "As ye would that others would do to you do ye even so to them" is the complete answer to all problems that can arise between people. The Christian philosophy of life is complete. Our reaction to it is the problem. We do not easily change our developed habits. The acceptance of such change is the problem, not the development of a proper program.

The first change in industry that would occur if we were to accept the Christian philosophy would be the elimination of present labor-management friction. That friction has reduced the efficiency of industrial production to a small fraction of what is easily possible with cooperation. Such efficiency is now being obtained in companies where cooperation has been achieved.

The second problem to be solved would be the unfairness of the taxing policy of government. At present, because of its preparation for war and its drift to socialism, our government is taking in taxes a very large part of the income of all people. Particularly is this true of those who are our industrial leaders and on whose leadership we must depend for economic advance.

When we consider the fact that the industrialist who owns a successful manufacturing company pays in general more than twice as much in taxes on the same income as any taxpayer outside of industry pays, the unfairness is evident.

The third change that would result would be the revamping of our ideas as to the reason for industry and the proper distribution of its earnings.

All of these problems are to some extent interdependent. If Christ's philosophy be adopted in our solution of one of them, the application of the same philosophy would solve all of them. The solution seems obvious. The acceptance of the solution is the problem. This has always been true of every step forward that man has ever taken. Change that is obviously desirable if one thinks about it objectively is difficult to effect, since habit hesitates to let us change, no matter how practical the change might be.

The effect of habit on our lives is tremendous. Most of our acts are controlled by habit. Few are the result of objective thinking and planning. A consideration of the effect of habit, therefore, is necessary, since it is carrying us in wrong directions.

Habits usually have little foundation in objective judgment. They generally are acts that were started for a proper reason. We are, however, apt to continue such acts after the reason for them has long since disappeared. From the selection of what we eat for breakfast to what political party we vote for, we largely follow habit. There is no doubt that following habit relieves us of much mental effort. Following habit, however, prevents progress. Progress is made only by doing the new and habitually unusual. Progress can be made in no other way.

One of the illustrations of the hold that habit has on us is so-called "daylight saving time." We wish in summer to be about in more of the daylight hours. Habit rebels against our getting up an hour earlier. Habit makes this hard to do. We can overcome the difficulty, however, by turning our watches ahead an hour. Since habit has taught us to do most things according to the position of the hands of our watches, we can by turning our watches ahead an hour do all things with the hands of the watch in the habitual place and still do them an hour earlier. The fact that this program of kidding ourselves results in many mistakes in meeting appointments and catching planes does not disturb us very much.

It is obvious that we could do all things without the present errors caused by kidding ourselves as to what time it actually is. All such deception would be eliminated if we would only leave our watches alone and do all things an hour earlier. But habit will not allow us to do that; the only way we can change our program is to have the hands of our watches in the usual position when we go through our daily routine.

We see the same hold that habit has on our thinking in the attitude of most white people toward Negroes. Many Negroes have abilities beyond those of the white men who decry them. In slavery days the Negro was thought of as little above an animal. Many still so think of him. This habit even extends toward those Negroes whose minds and characters merit high respect and admiration. And it is still true when the Negro is almost completely white.

We see the same attitude in some bosses toward their men in industry. Every worker in the shop has abilities that the boss does not have. These abilities are essential if the business is to succeed. Yet the boss often looks down on the wage earner in his own mind and in his treatment of him. This attitude is again the result of habit. A generation ago the boss actually was in a dominant position. He often had greater knowledge, skill and experience than the worker. But that time has largely passed in present-day industry. The worker today is an expert who has abilities that are far beyond the boss's. His contribution is completely necessary if industry is to succeed and progress.

We see the same hold of habit in the respect that is paid to royalty. The king now in most countries is a figurehead with no power and no responsibility. He is still revered by his subjects, however, as he was five-hundred years ago when he had power and shaped the future of his people. Here again habit controls actions when reason might do otherwise.

Habit also differentiates classes. The routines that are followed in eating, talking and dressing classify the individual in the minds of many people. Acceptance depends in many cases on what habits have been de-

25

veloped and how they are followed. The habits involved and the resulting acceptance or rejection usually have no relation to the ability of the individual. The reaction of his contemporaries, however, is often dependent on these inconsequential actions. All these examples merely illustrate how our actions and conclusions are affected by habit, rather than by reason.

Often habit will cause us to come to conclusions that have no basis in actual fact. In coming to these conclusions, we often do not consider objectively the facts involved. We do not try to think the matter through. We accept what is believed by those with whom we associate. We go no farther. This of course relieves us of much mental effort. It also saves us from being considered peculiar. But it is death to progress. All progress must be different from that which has gone before. It cannot be actual progress unless it is different.

It was not until after his crucifixion that anyone, including the disciples, really recognized the greatness of Jesus. The mob crucified him with little objection. Perhaps we ourselves should not have acted any differently than the mob did at the time of the crucifixion. We often do not recognize greatness when we come in contact with it.

It is only after we accept and benefit by the progress that a genius makes, that we recognize his greatness. The acceptance usually comes later when we have had a chance to forget our previous resistance to his new ideas.

Most people resist progress, since to habit-controlled

minds it is not progress but only error. We resisted the automobile, the bath tub, the water closet and the railroad, when first developed, to mention only a few. We could not believe that they were steps forward, since they were different from our previous ways.

There are always a few who urge the new and different. The difficulty is that the majority do not go along. This hesitation may be based on the selfish interests of those who will be hurt by such progress. But in most cases we resist change because it disturbs and upsets our habitual way of life.

Such resistance to change is well illustrated currently by the preparation for war that takes a large part of the energies and incomes of all the people on earth. Everyone knows that an atomic war such as we are preparing for would mean the end of civilization. Those who would not die would live in an economy that would be barbaric and terrible. Those who would be killed would be fortunate by comparison. No reasonable person could follow such a program of national suicide. If an individual should prepare for suicide as the governments are now doing we would put him into an asylum. No government would prepare for war if men would follow objective reasoning. However, men have always gone to war as a means of settling differences between nations. We, therefore, because of habit, will not follow any other method in our relationships with the rest of the world.

Eventually, we must follow a different and reasonable course if we are to continue to exist. The power of destruction that has been developed by man can no longer be safely left to previous habit. We must develop a new philosophy. Because war is outmoded, the war habit must be changed. It will be changed either after we destroy most people, which we are now preparing to do, or we will by objective reasoning come to the proper conclusion. War is now too efficient to use, no matter how habitual it has been heretofore.

The proper solution has been given to us, and we say that we accept that solution when we call ourselves Christians. Christ in his ministry on earth gave us a Christian philosophy which we profess to believe in and which could solve our problems. But we should have some difficulty in showing that we follow Christ's teaching in our present habitual actions, not only because of our war preparation, but also by our actions in many other fields. Because of habit, this philosophy of Christ is accepted only as theory. We will not govern our lives by his principles. They are for Sunday only; not for the rest of the week.

The Christian philosophy is only useful when it is applied as the guiding principle of our everyday lives. There is no point in calling ourselves Christians, as we do, and then refusing to follow the philosophy of Christ. That would be in the same category as believing that air is necessary to life, but refusing to breathe.

With our present fear of the communist nations, our hesitation to follow the Christian ethic, and our war habit, it is perhaps useless to suggest that we follow the Christian philosophy in regard to war. Perhaps we are not developed far enough to accept Christ's teachings in dealing with other nations. There are, however, other places where we can apply the Christian ethic where habit is not as controlling as it is in our international dealing.

Habit does not interfere with solving the problem of labor-management relations to the same extent as it does our tendency to go to war when we disagree with other nations. The policy of "all the traffic will bear" also is not completely ingrained in us. We can in industry, perhaps, apply the Christian ethic without too great resistance from our habit patterns.

How, then, can we get cooperation between so-called labor and so-called management? Unquestionably the ethics of Christ will achieve it, as has been found by every company where this philosophy has been applied. What would happen if we should apply the philosophy of the Sermon on the Mount to this relationship? Such application has been made and the answer given has been demonstrated over many years. Let us see just what would happen.

First: Efficiency in production increases enormously. This is the result of *desire* on the part of the worker to be efficient. It also results in the development by the worker of new techniques, new methods, new machines, new designs and also the development of new abilities in the worker himself.

Second: Because of this increased efficiency, the cost of the products made is rapidly and continuously reduced. This reduction in cost, after properly rewarding those who accomplish it, is passed on to the customer in lower prices and a continuously better and better product.

Third: Since the wish to make the product better in design and lower in cost is the desire of all involved, there will be continuous development of the latent abilities of all those who are responsible for this progress in the company. They will all as a consequence be progressively more able, more productive and more efficient. They will constantly increase in individual stature.

Fourth: The worker will be continuously employed. This will eliminate his fear of the future, which now makes him resist progress in efficiency. It will also make industry and consequently the economy much more stable. Progress will be continuous. Our present records of production will be far outdistanced. Booms and slumps such as are now usual will not occur.

Perhaps we think that the above outline is only good in theory. That is not so. Every time the Christian ethic has been applied in industry, such results have been achieved. There are some companies that have followed the philosophy of Christ in their industrial program; the results obtained are the measure of how closely the philosophy is followed. The following example is indicative.

A manufacturing company in the electrical industry —the Lincoln Electric Company—started to apply a

Christian program in its dealings with its workers and customers twenty-six years ago. Since that time, the manhours per unit of production have been reduced by more than 90%. Its prices to the customer as an average have not increased, in spite of the fact that labor costs per hour are many times what they were twenty-six years ago and the raw materials used that are furnished by outside suppliers have increased in price more than three times. In spite of these cost increases, the profit per dollar of sales has remained constant during that period with no average increase in price of the products that the company makes. (This record is shown in the Appendix.)

This outcome is natural whenever those involved follow the precepts of the Master. The cooperation of the worker and the customer is automatic. Success is assured. The only problem that is inherent in the program is to break habits that are now customary in industry in management's dealing with the customer and the worker. That is the only difficulty. It is hard because of habit to treat the worker as a fellow member of the team and reward him proportionately. It is hard to give the customer more than we must. Habit is hard to break.

We call ourselves Christians. We admit that to be Christian means that we follow the philosophy of Jesus Christ. However, we make continual exceptions whenever we think his teachings are contrary to our present interests. We are a Christian nation when we think Christianity will be good for us right now. We are very apt to steer away from the teachings of Jesus otherwise.

What Christ taught in his ministry on earth is not only a set of principles. It is a basic doctrine that is as completely necessary in our daily operations as are the natural laws of gravity and the multiplication tables.

2

Labor-Management
Problem Stated

I F W E will view objectively the problem of labor-management relations, we will eliminate many of the conclusions that have been habitual in our thinking. We then will have a completely different understanding of the problem. The interests of labor, management and the customer are identical in the final analysis. They are the same people ultimately. Why, then, do we have the continual friction between them that now prevails, with the penalty of a much lower standard of living for all?

The people involved are intelligent and patriotic. Their desire is for a better life. This can be obtained only by cooperation. They all know this; yet labor and

33

management are continually at war with each other. They do not cooperate to increase efficiency. They do just the opposite. Featherbedding and make-work schemes are the usual workers' program. When cooperation is actual, as has been true in a few cases, production efficiency many times that now usual in industry is automatic. Why is cooperation not obtained in all cases? That is the first problem that must be solved in developing a better economy.

There have been many attempts of various kinds to procure the cooperation of labor with management. Many of these programs are based on the idea that paying more money for more work will get such cooperation. Other programs derive from the idea that if some part of the profit of the company is given to the workers, cooperation will result. Still other industrialists feel that annuities or other fringe benefits will answer the problem.

All such programs have had beneficial results in some cases, but disastrous results in others. Cooperation is not necessarily the result of any plan. Man is too complex for that. Cooperation can be obtained only when all those involved in the operation desire to cooperate. If this mutual desire does not exist, cooperation will not result, no matter what incentive programs are used.

The workers' reaction to the program that management may initiate will determine the results obtained. The form or kind of plan does not itself determine the attitude of the wage earner. The same plan can and does produce diametrically opposite results in different companies. The plan is not conclusive. The attitude that the men involved have toward the plan is the completely determining factor.

We are very apt to think that paying more money to accomplish some desired end will produce cooperation toward achieving that end. That is not true. There are many incentives far more effective than money. For example Messrs. Wilson and MacNamara both gave up millions of dollars of income to take the post of Secretary of Defense at $25,000 per year. Status here is a much greater incentive than money.

The amateur athlete usually tries harder than the professional; he gets no money. Here too, status and self-respect are far greater incentives than money. The fact that money is not as great an incentive as other things is very necessary to remember, if we are to understand the problem of more efficient production by the worker.

When we approach the matter objectively, we see that industry as now usually operated can result only in the desire of the wage earner to resist efficient operation. He does not want greater efficiency. He wants just the opposite. His desire and need is to spin the job out.

It is safe to state that if those who cry loudest about the inefficiencies of labor were to be put in the position of the wage earner, they would react exactly as the present wage earner does. The worker is not a man apart. He has the same needs, aspirations and reactions as have the industrialists who now rail against him.

35

We industrialists want greater efficiency from the worker. This is well within his ability. And production rates many times those of the present are very easily obtained when the workers *want* to cooperate. The present policies of industrial managers, however, penalize such efficiency or any move toward it. Obviously, a worker will not cooperate on any program that will penalize him. Does any manager?

The greatest fear of the worker, which is the same as the greatest fear of the industrialist in operating a company, is lack of income. The policy of industrial management is controlled by a program that will in the opinion of management assure continuous profit. All industrial plants are controlled by this need. The wage earner has the same necessity and a more personal one than has the industrialist. That necessity also controls his actions. The industrial manager is very conscious of his company's need of uninterrupted income. He is completely oblivious, evidently, of the fact that the worker has exactly the same need. The worker's fear of no income is far more intense than the industrialist's, since his daily bread and that of his family depend on his job. The industrialist would not miss a meal if his company should run at a loss for a length of time equal to that for which the worker was laid off because of lack of orders.

In spite of these facts, the industrialist will fire the worker any time he feels that he can get along without him. The worker has no control over his future. His need of continuous income is far more urgent than that

36

of management, yet he has no recourse. Only management is responsible for the loss of the worker's job. Only management can follow and develop a program that will bring in orders. The worker can't. Management, which is responsible, keeps its job. The man who had no responsibility is thrown out. Management failed in its job and had no punishment. The wage earner did not fail in his job but was fired. No man will go along with such injustice, nor should he. This is still true, in spite of custom which completely sanctions such procedure.

It is obvious that higher efficiency in any operation means that it will take fewer manhours to do it. If as a result the worker loses his job more quickly (as he does now) there is no doubt that he will oppose any plan that will produce greater efficiency. This would be equally true of the industrialist if he were to be put in the wage earner's place.

The second problem that must be solved by management, if the efficiency inherent in man is to be achieved, is the division of the greatly increased profit resulting from greater efficiency. There never will be much enthusiasm for greater efficiency—in the minds of those who produce the efficiency—even if job security is achieved, if the profit from greater efficiency is not properly distributed.

Greater efficiency, resulting from cooperation of labor and management, cannot be achieved if, in the worker's opinion, the profit from such achievement is not properly used. Here again, the industrialist should put himself in the wage earner's place and see what his own reaction would be. If we are to get greater efficiency from greater cooperation, we must follow a new and different course in profit distribution from that which is now usual.

Continuous employment is the first step to efficiency. This will remove the fear now present in the worker's mind. We must then have a proper use, in the worker's thinking, for the far greater profit that results from such efficiency.

If we continue present custom in the distribution of profit, that is, give it to the average stockholder, who did nothing to make it, the producers of these greater profits will not cooperate. We must have new thinking. There are two groups who must be rewarded by such profits. They are, first, the workers, from top to bottom, who increased the profit by their skill and cooperation. Second, of equal importance, is the customer. He paid for all the costs of production and all profit. He is the only reason that industry exists. Rewarding him must be a prime consideration, since industry could not exist without his buying. He is the only reason for industry.

The last group to be considered is the stockholders who own stock because they think it will be more profitable than investing money in any other way. The stockholder, as listed here, is not the man who is the owner or who founded the business or supplied the original capital. Such founding owners usually are actual producers and should be so considered. But the absentee stockholder is not of any value to the customer or the worker, since he has no knowledge of nor interest in the company other than greater dividends and an advance in the price of his stock.

How each of these groups should be rewarded is a problem that management must resolve. It must be done in such a way that labor, management and the customer all feel that a proper distribution has been made. Only so will they cooperate.

There must be complete honesty and understanding between the hourly worker and management if high efficiency is to be obtained. Here again we cannot safely follow custom. It is present custom that has made present inefficiency. We must change this custom.

When industrial management makes industry attractive, useful and helpful to the worker (and to the customer) in a way that the worker feels is justified, he will cooperate and industrial efficiency will increase at an unbelievable rate compared to what it is now. Such results have always occurred when such cooperation has been obtained.

Management's benighted policy in dealing with the worker has been responsible for the present grave crisis that exists in labor-management relations. A great opportunity for advance in understanding has been completely botched. The worker has had to go to the union to get the increase in standard of living and status that he should have gotten from management automatically. He has been forced by management's continued resistance to progress through the union. That is how the present war between labor and management developed.

The progress that the hourly worker has made, both in status and income, which has been resisted by the usual industrial management, is completely necessary to the progress of the economy. If the income of the hourly worker were the same now as it was a generation ago, industry as we know it now could not exist. Most of the buying on which industry as now organized depends is done by the hourly worker. If he did not do such buying, most present manufacturing would disappear, since there would be no market for its products. How many automobiles, houses and furnishings would be bought if the hourly worker got twenty cents per hour or less, as he did a generation or so ago?

The financial progress of the hourly worker is completely necessary to the economy. The industrial managers, however, in most cases have resisted every step forward that has been taken by the worker. If industrial management had taken the lead in giving to the worker the reward he now has, as it should have done, the problem of labor-management friction never would have developed. Labor unions as now organized would not exist. The present friction would not have developed.

It is obvious that the worker and the manager are the same kind of people fundamentally, even though they have different abilities. The worker has the same aspirations as the manager. Management resisted the worker's attempt to make progress. The worker rebelled. This rebellion was organized by forming unions which brought the workers of each craft into a group. Each union had the power to shut down industry by striking. A new kind of war was developed. As is true of all wars, it resulted in destruction to those involved as well as to the rest of the economy. It was effective in eliminating management's previous domination over the worker, however. As a result, the worker got a greater increase in status and income from the industry involved. His buying has made the economy advance to where it now is.

If wages should return to the rates that were usual a generation ago, chaos would result in industry. Much of the buying now done by the hourly worker would disappear. Industry would disappear to the same extent, since there would be less of its output needed. The economy would be a small fraction of what it is now. Present prosperity would disappear. The standard of living would be far lower than that to which we are now accustomed. All would suffer from such a tragedy. All industrialists want present buying to continue. In spite of these facts, most industrialists have fought every reward that the worker has received, and still do.

Instead of fighting labor's progress, suppose that management had cooperated with the worker. What would then have been the result? First of all, the position of management in the worker's mind would be completely different. The hourly worker, instead of fighting management, would give it his complete loyalty. Instead of friction, there would be cooperation. Instead of disputes, there would be harmony. Instead

41

of restriction of output, there would be tremendous increase of efficiency. The standard of living of all would be far ahead of what it is now.

If management had cooperated in labor's advance, the wage rates would be the same as now. Fringe benefits would be the same as now. The leadership of management, however, would be unquestioned and because of that, the efficiency of industry would be far beyond what is now usual. Foreign competition, which presently threatens our industrial future, would be largely eliminated, since we would by our efficiency outstrip it.

This is not theory. This program of cooperation has been obtained by some manufacturers. The results are as might be expected. There is no foreign competition for their products in this country. There is, instead, the sale of products made by such cooperation to countries throughout the world.

But this result comes not only from cooperation between labor and management. The cause is much deeper than actual cooperation in working. When the workers in any industrial organization really want to make the company more successful, many advantages flow from that desire. There is not only the elimination of friction, but also the development of men, techniques, machines and methods, which enormously reduces costs while it improves the product. Such vigorous progress within an industry is far more important in reducing costs than the mere elimination of friction.

Cooperation between labor and management must be accomplished if we are to retain our present position in the family of nations. We are rapidly losing our place now in competition with manufacturers in Europe and Asia. If this continues as it is now going, we soon will be outdistanced.

There is all the potential ability needed in our workers and our management for us to continue to be world leaders in production. We need only have the cooperation that is possible and now obtained by forward-looking companies to have our country's industry remain supreme.

It is well in our approach to this problem of cooperation to recognize the unreality of our present government-regulated, labor-management programs. We have what we call collective bargaining to settle the terms of agreement in labor-management relations. If we will look at the matter objectively, we shall see that such an approach is completely unreal. There is no possibility of proper bargaining between labor and management. The customer, who is not even being considered and who pays all costs of production, is the proper bargainer. Labor and management are on the same team. The only one with whom bargaining should take place, labor and management being on the same side of the table, is the customer. Since the customer pays all wages, fringe benefits and the cost of feather-bedding, as well as all other costs of production, he is the one to bargain with the labor-management team.

Neither management nor the union has any right to say what the customer should pay to the worker. If we should deal with reality, collective bargaining would be far different from present custom. The customer would determine all labor-management rewards, based on efficiency of production.

With our present program of collective bargaining, management and labor together determine how much the customer will pay for the worker's remuneration and for his inefficiencies. The customer, who pays all costs, is not even consulted. It is not strange that the results from such irresponsible bargaining should be disappointing and often foolish, as we now see.

In the final analysis, the purpose of industry is to supply the public with the products it needs and wants. This public includes the worker as well as management, plus all other people. Any wrong development in industry, be it improper design, too costly products, inefficient production or featherbedding, is paid for by the customers, who, of course, include labor and management. Inefficiency from any source is paid for by the buyer. Here again we must eliminate habit and deal with reality. Here again, habit has distorted our present vision. A new view must be taken, and soon. There is no single step that is more important to the future of our economy than the solution of this labor-management problem. It will obviously take new thinking and a new approach. Once more we must apply the philosophy of Christ in his Sermon on the Mount. That would eliminate the problem and give a solution that cannot fail.

3

Industrial Organization

I NDUSTRY and its operation, together with its goals, have been changed greatly by the policies of government and its program of taxation. The previous money incentive for the industrialist has been eliminated by the present taxation at steeply punitive rates. Because of this, many companies have been sold by their founders into industrial complexes which are operated by hired managers who have little ownership and little control of fundamental policy, such as the original owner had.

These changes in management have had great effect on the present operation of industry. The effect will be progressively greater in the future as the concentration of ownership proceeds. The previous owner had full authority. The present hired manager does not. He is under the control of the stockholders through their board of directors. His policy is largely controlled by others. The goal of the company, because of the change of ownership and policy, has gone largely from service to the customer, and making a better and better product at a lower and lower price, to larger dividends for the stockholders.

This change is not because the stockholder is more selfish than the previous owner was. It is because the new management does not, and perhaps cannot, change from the profit goal. The larger the organization, the more it is controlled in policy by previous custom and the less by new and progressive thinking and planning.

We see this fact illustrated in the program of pricing done by large industry. Competition has little control over price. That is controlled by management. Deviation from standard pricing is not considered healthy. It is not done.

When industry was controlled by privately owned companies, competition largely ruled prices. Prices were not standardized. But power is now concentrated in a few hands and prices are standardized. We see this demonstrated when we compare the changes in the prices of steel, copper, aluminum and many of the plastics, which are produced by large organizations, with the changes of prices of the manufactured products made from these same materials which are usually made by smaller competitive companies.

A good case can be made for such controlled prices. The European manufacturers have always done this to a great extent and are sure their program is right. But the great difficulty with such policies is that the competitive pressures toward lower prices disappear and progress in development of the product is reduced. The pressure of competition is largely gone.

The proper responsibility of industry is to build a better and better product at a lower and lower price. That will be the goal of industry if it is controlled by competition. That also would be the goal if it were controlled by Christian philosophy. In either case, the pressure to make progress by competition in industry as originally operated will be great and continuous. This need and pressure can be reduced by price agreements or by controlled prices. There is much temptation for the less willing and less expert operators to sidestep their responsibility and needed effort by getting the high prices that can be made standard for the industry by agreement. Such a policy has been followed largely in Europe, where it can be done legally. The same program has been followed here to a less extent and less openly, since it is illegal.

A very apt illustration of such change in management's methods and goals is in the operation of the Ford Motor Company under Henry Ford the 1st, and now. The price of the original Ford car went continually down from 1908 to 1928, from $950 to $290. The present Ford car has gone continually *up* in price. This is largely the result of the change of goal that management had under Henry Ford the first and now. This same goal is generally controlling in all large industry, as now operated.

This program of price increase is to some extent necessary under the present tax program of government. Since the greater part of all profit that industry makes is taken by government the price must be high enough to cover the tax take. It cannot be paid in any other way. Prices therefore must be made higher than they were previously to cover this charge. That is one reason why the price of cars is higher now than when Ford the 1st largely controlled the automobile market.

How this tax policy affects the economy can be realized now that so many feel that if taxes were reduced prosperity would increase. The administration is told that a tax reduction would immediately promote prosperity and hence re-employ the idle workers. If that were true can one imagine the prosperity that we would have if we had had the tax program that was in force at the beginning of the century.

There is no known limit to the cost reductions that can be made in the manufacture of any product if cost reduction is the actual goal of both management and men. But that goal is largely changed to profits and dividends when the hired manager is under the direction of the stockholder, as is now usual in large, complex corporations.

Industry, if efficient, involves very complicated operations. There is no activity that is more difficult than the progressively efficient operation of a manufacturing company. It is because of its many and completely diverse problems requiring successful handling that there are so few continuously successful industrial managers where competition controls prices. Because of this and the present taxation program, most industrial organizations fail, disappear or are sold within a generation.

Perhaps the reason why the successful industrialist is continually discounted by government and the public is because industry is so complicated that it is not understood generally. Its problems, its needs and its responsibilities are not known by those outside. The public—ignorant of the complexities of industry—does not properly evaluate the genius of successful industrial leadership when it does occur.

The public recognizes a successful professional baseball player as being one in a thousand. The same public, however, does not recognize that the successful industrialist is a much rarer individual. If and when we do understand this, there will be a new and completely different attitude toward the industrialist by the voter, and consequently by government.

The industrial manager can overcome most of his difficulties if he has no competition. This may be accomplished by price agreements or cartels, which are usual in Europe, but legislated against here. The chief problems and difficulties that the successful manager must face are present only when competition is controlling. This is less and less true when price is partially or completely controlled by agreements. Competition also

49

becomes less of an element as size increases. Prices are more stable and more easily raised when large companies dominate the field. The industrialist of whom we are now thinking is controlled by competition. There are still many such. All new industry is managed by such people.

The industrialist, to be successful in a competitive economy, must first develop products that will be bought as against competing products. This is no small job. More than a thousand automobile manufacturers have tried, failed, and disappeared because they could not do it. Only a few successful manufacturers of automobiles are left. The industrialist, to be successful after developing a desirable product, must then produce it at a price at which it will profitably sell in competition with all other products. That too, is no easy job, as is evidenced by the concerns that fail because their costs are too high.

The successful industrialist then has just started. He must continually reduce costs. Only so can he progress. In doing that, the most important step is to get the cooperation of his organization. Here again is one cause of the failure of the thousands of concerns which disappear every year. Union leadership now backed by government has greatly restricted such cooperation. Restriction of efficiency by dominant union leadership has stopped and even reversed efficiency in many manufacturing plants. The unions have not cooperated in cost reduction in spite of the need of the economy for such progress.

50

The public will not yet believe that our standard of living could be more than doubled immediately if labor and management would cooperate rather than fight as they do now, and so reduce costs and the consequent selling prices.

The fact that there has been progress of nearly three percent per year in efficiency of American industrial productivity in spite of such resistance shows that the industrialist in many cases has made a marvelous contribution to our economic progress.

The industrialist to succeed also must deal successfully with the consumer's prejudices. He must give to him a constantly better product in spite of the consumer's resistance to the changes necessary to make a better product. The automobile was resisted by both law and custom for a long time. It was only many years after its introduction that the user found that he must have it. The same resistance has retarded all progress. The consumer will not accept progress easily.

The industrialist also must obtain progressively better materials if progress is to be made. Here the knowledge of the scientist and the judgment of the realist must be fused. If he fails here, his success will be questionable.

The last problem that the industrialist must face is the attitude of government toward success in industry. His own present profits are taxed at more than twice the rate that any other income is taxed.

All industrial profits are first taxed 52%. After that tax has been levied, there is the usual income tax up to

51

91% levied on all income taken by the owner either as salary or dividends from his operation. It is only recently that another tax of 30% on some profits was removed. This was called an excess profits tax. It made the 52% tax on profits more like 70%.

This punitive tax program is having and will continue to have a tremendous effect on the future operation of industry. Since the successful industrialist can more than double his income if he will sell out and invest in other activities, that is the program often followed by company founders. It is particularly true when the owner approaches the end of his active life.

It is evident that this punitive program is the result of a desire on the part of the public to punish industrial success. It is the natural reaction of mediocrity to genius. The average always wants to pull down the able to the level of the average. We see this not only in the punitive taxation of the able in industry but also in the attitude of the union to the skilled worker. It is the program of the union to tend to equalize the income of the common laborer and the skilled worker. Excellence is always decried by the average and perhaps always will be.

Constantly increasing industrial efficiency is necessary to progress. Yet the government penalizes rather than rewards those who produce it. The industrialist is in somewhat the same position as the slave was a hundred years ago. He was completely necessary, since the master could not live without him, but he was despised and exploited by the same master. The industrialist in like manner is completely necessary to the public. However, if he is successful he is held up to continuous criticism and punished by our unequal tax laws for his success. This program may punish the successful as is planned by the less successful, but its results are suicidal to the future of the economy.

Industry also is regulated by law in a way that no other activity is regulated. Combinations of companies, methods of distribution, advertising, tariffs on imports and control of exports are subject to governmental regulation. The contacts of industrialists with each other are controlled by law to an extent that would cause revolution if applied to all people. We apply the authority of the dictator to industry. Freedom of action is for those outside industry.

What the eventual effect of such unfair treatment of the industrialist will be is still to be seen. American government has never before penalized the able for their ability. There are certain results of this already, that may indicate the future. The industrial genius has largely stopped trying. He has sold out and gone to vacation lands to loaf, rather than expose himself to the present punishment for success. Why should an owner try, when progressively stiffer punishment for success is the result? He can sell out and so escape punitive taxation. By so doing he can also increase his income.

This penalizing of the successful industrialist is of small consequence as far as the unfairness itself is concerned. The number of successful industrialists is small. The number who are wronged will have little effect on the attitude of the rest of the people. There are many examples of a majority, by their power, exploiting a minority. That is not the great danger.

The problem that we face is the effect that this program will have on the attitude of the industrial genius of the future, on whose ability our future prosperity so completely depends. Can we get along successfully without him and his leadership in industry? What will be the effect on the economy when he quits, as he is now being forced to do? How will we meet the competition of communism where genius *is* highly rewarded?

As the rare geniuses that are in industry disappear, the economy will be greatly changed by their absence. The individual owner and operator of an industry has an entirely different outlook and goal for his company than the hired managers who operate the large and complex organizations, which are the result of the present combinations of smaller companies that have been absorbed.

The wholly-owned company under the direction of its founder has a different approach to profit, price, progress and attitude toward the customer than the hired manager is allowed to take by his board of directors. The latter is usually directed to make greater profit for the stockholders his goal. There is no other end in view. But the wholly-owned company that is operated by its founder often has a different concept.

There the founder is looking for the new, the unusual and the progressive. He also is not under the control of absentee stockholders who have little knowledge of the company aside from its dividends.

Industry's goal, if it is to succeed as it can, must be completely different from simply increasing dividends. Industry controls our standard of living. We cannot allow it to be converted to a source of profit only for a limited number of non-producing people. The small company under the leadership of the individual industrial genius is the source of most progress in both the quality and price of manufactured products. The industrial genius must be encouraged to continue in this program. We must encourage him to remain the leader. We must not discourage him, as our present tax policy has done and is doing.

The industrial competition of communism, which can only be met by more efficient production, will be far surpassed by the development that is inherent in free competitive industry if we will encourage, not penalize, accomplishment.

When we encourage rather than punish success in industry, the genius, who alone can make progress, will develop and lead our industry to new and greater heights. Such genius does not develop under dictatorship. No Edison or Kettering can be developed by the command of a Khrushchev or Stalin. Such genius develops only in an atmosphere of freedom. That is our advantage over communism if we will exploit it.

The answer is simple and obvious. We need only follow it. Man has endless abilities if we will only recognize the fact and encourage him to develop himself. He will then develop a continually greater economy.

4

Pricing and Cutting Prices

WHAT should be the goal for the industrialist in his operation of an industry? The one often followed is that of producing a maximum profit. The method generally used is to charge the highest price that can be got from the customer. In many cases the price charged depends on how much or how little price pressure is put on the manufacturer by the customer. If the customer puts no pressure on price, he is charged the maximum. If he puts sufficient pressure on the manufacturer, he frequently pays much less. The asking price is only a hope in the mind of many producers. The actual price that is finally accepted may be much less.

Such an approach to the customer should and does condemn the manufacturer in the customer's mind. The buyer, when he finally agrees on a price, is sure in his own mind that if he had tried harder and longer a still lower price could have been obtained. He still feels that he has been robbed. He looks on the supplier as a potential crook, who in spite of the cut price charged more than he would charge if he had been honest.

It is true that price cutting is a customary practice. That does not make it honest. There are many popular crimes, such as price agreements and speeding. Custom may reduce condemnation, but it does not make a dishonest act honest.

If the producer can cut the price in one case, he should do it in all cases. Reducing prices should be a never ending manufacturer's policy. He should do it because he is continually reducing costs which of course will make price reduction in the same scale the proper way to operate a manufacturing company. It should never simply be a dodge to get an order.

Any manufacturer must be an expert in his line. He should be able to lead the customer in the direction that the customer should go in the use of his product. In doing this, price, quality and proper application are the seller's responsibility. He must eventually accept it and carry it out as an expert and as an honest man.

This is now far from customary. Again, habit has warped our character. We do not ask the proper price at first. That price is often far beyond what it should be. When we can sell no more at that price, a clearance sale at a fraction of the previous asking price is put on. If that price is proper then, it was proper at all times. If it is wrong, then it was improper always.

Habit has warped our ideas on many subjects. In the matter of distribution and the methods used, custom has taken us far from reality. When we consider that the cost of distribution of all the things we buy is far greater as an average than the cost of production, we have a measure of how far we have gone from the proper policy.

The reason for this lack of a proper pricing program is the habit that has been built up over the ages. Selling formerly was a game in which the buyer and seller matched wits. Honesty had no place in such bargaining. The seller got the highest price he could, regardless of value. The buyer protected himself as well as he could by any means at his disposal. Value had little effect on price. Price was solely a game of wits.

As the economy grew, the seller became a company instead of a person. The proprietor of such organizations found that his salesmen were not as expert at bargaining as he was. Because of that, the proprietor had to stop bargaining in selling, as it had become a losing game. The seller had to have one price, at least at one time. When goods were not bought, however, he had to cut the price in order to sell them. He could not return to bargaining, because customers might outmaneuver his salesmen. Therefore, the proprietor set the new and lower price. In a free market there never has been any way of holding prices artificially high. Even-

59

tually the prices of products which are wrongly priced must be cut to meet competition after the higher asking prices eliminate many customers.

We see the same philosophy in much advertising. It is safe to say that few people believe any advertisement. Few advertisements are meant to be believed. The advertiser does not expect readers to believe what he says. If he thought that he could get the reader to believe what he said, his advertising would be far different. At the present state of distribution, advertising is for the purpose of getting a name and a product made by the named company into the fleeting attention of the purchaser.

The advertiser knows that the buyer has little knowledge of the products in any field. He therefore feels that if he can get the buyer to remember his name in his field, the customer will almost automatically buy the product that he remembers. There is no doubt that the scheme works. If the customer does not remember the name of the product that he ought to buy, he will seldom buy it. This is still true when the advertised product must have charged against it all of the cost of advertising and therefore is higher in price than a product available, but unknown to the customer, at a lower price.

It is obvious that if all customers knew all the facts regarding all the things that they buy, there would be a complete change in the methods of marketing. There also would be a tremendous lowering of the prices that the customer would have to pay. The cost of distribution would be only a small part of the total cost of products bought, rather than the largest part, as is true now.

The mail order houses have made some progress toward this more efficient distribution. The reputation of these organizations for honesty and fairness has advanced their position in the thinking of the customer. There are handicaps to the operation of such organizations because of distance and habit. Their position in the minds of the public is constantly getting better, however. This is the result of a small step in the direction of more economical distribution. It is only a small start, however.

The elimination of the previous bargaining in arriving at the selling price has also been a step forward, where it occurs. Bargaining is still common in the distribution of many products where the policy of having an asking price that will be reduced under pressure is still customary. In the case of large-industry control of the market, the price that is set is much less apt to be cut than in fully competitive industry. That is still true when the price is artificially high. Competition is controlled. Price reduction is not done.

The habits followed in distribution, which are largely controlling, are perhaps more costly to the economy than any other habits in industry. They are far more wasteful in their final effect on cost than even the waste generated by labor-management friction, although they are less evident. However, the solution to the distribution problem is the same as the solution to all the difficulties that man has in his contact with other people.

If we should apply the Christian philosophy to the problem, the result would be as rewarding to all concerned as it is in all other application. Custom so far has not allowed us to do this, even with its great reward. As so often is true, habit has eliminated such progress.

It is unfortunate that so many of us have been taught that Christianity and its precepts, if followed, are the means of keeping ourselves from going to hell. This was the idea that the churches formerly stressed. Today, most of us are not as afraid of hell as our ancestors were and the teachings of Christ do not attract us as a means of escaping from eternal tortures. But too few of us realize fully that the Christian philosophy actually is the best known way of living successfully on this earth. It is the practical philosophy of everyday life. The closer we come to following Christ's precepts, the more successful we will be in solving our problems.

This will still be true if the present church religious programs are entirely forgotten. Christ teaches a plan of success in everyday life. There is no other known way of life that can succeed so completely. It successfully answers all the problems that man can face in his life on earth.

The great difficulty in our concept of religion is that we think of it as a theory that has little application to everyday living. We think of it as an ideal program that we revere but do not apply to practical affairs. Christianity in the usual mind is like a diet or health program that we read about. We think it is applicable only under unusual circumstances, when we are sick, or fat, or injured. We do not think it is usable now, right at this moment. We are getting along all right following custom. We are content to let well enough alone. Christianity is something we will perhaps apply later when we feel we are in some trouble that overwhelms us.

In fact, Christianity is instead the only successful program for everyday life. When used, it answers all our problems in all our daily relationships with each other.

A very good illustration of the proper application of the Christian precept was the program that Gandhi followed in obtaining the freedom of India from England. Gandhi applied the philosophy of Christ to the problem. India became free. If Gandhi had applied the usual method of gaining freedom a war would have been fought and the result would have been questionable and in any case ruinous to both England and India.

It is interesting to note that Gandhi in his leadership was respected much less by the public than Churchill or Roosevelt, who applied the usual methods in settling disputes between nations. Habit in our acts and thoughts is hard to change.

If the Christian ethic were followed in distribution, the first step would be complete honesty in our contact with the customer. The manufacturer is the expert in his line. It is his responsibility to give to the customer the best thing that is available for his needs. The seller has this responsibility because he is the expert and honesty requires him to tell the buyer the whole truth. When the seller knows the buyer's problem, perhaps he may not have the best thing for the need of that buyer. It is still the seller's responsibility to direct the customer to the proper thing for his needs. This is equally true if the proper thing has to come from the seller's competitor.

All acts of the seller should be controlled by this principle. This would be true of advertising and any other publicity. The Christian ethic should control our acts. If it did control our acts, the savings in costs of distribution would be tremendous. Advertising would be truthful education only. Selling would be a contact of the expert consultant with the customer, in order to give the customer the best product available when all of the customer's needs are considered. Competition then would be in improving the quality of products and increasing efficiency in producing and distributing them; not in deception, as is now too customary. Pricing would reflect efficiency of production; it would not be a selling dodge that the customer may well be sorry he accepted. It would be proper for all concerned and rewarding for the ability used in producing the product.

This program is a far cry from what is now usual. The experience of the few industrialists who follow the teachings of Christ has shown, however, that Christianity is the only continually successful program that can be followed. It answers all the problems that any industry has, as their experience is continually proving.

When industry follows the Christian philosophy,

some obvious changes will be made in our economy. Salesmen will change from peddlers to consultants. Their number will greatly decrease. Advertising will be changed from deception to instruction and it will also decrease in volume. The reputation of a product will be determined not by the quantity of money spent in advertising it, but by its actual use to the customer. The facts about the product will be announced in the same way that other scientific progress is publicized. With such a program, the cost of distribution in relation to sales will be a small fraction of what is usual now.

Advertising would show and celebrate the real progress made in industry. It would keep the public up to date. This is a far cry from what is done now.

5

Labor-Management
Solution Outlined

I F W E are to get full cooperation of labor
and management in industrial production, there must
be a radical change from the present relationship.
Such a change will be difficult to get because of past
habits.

Both workers and managers must realize completely
that their progress can only come from willing cooperation.

"Cooperation," as used here, does not mean just the
elimination of resistance to progress in efficiency. That
is of small importance. Cooperation is the working together of all people in the organization in the same way
that all the members of an athletic team work together

to win a game. Cooperation does not mean elimination of featherbedding only. It means the enthusiastic finding of new methods, new tools, new ideas, by all people, from top to bottom in the organization. Cooperation means the enthusiastic use by all people in the company of their best ideas, skills and methods to reduce costs and improve quality in any way that can be done.

Such cooperation is present in athletics. It is present in the family. It is present in much top management. It is not present in the usual labor-management relations. When cooperation such as outlined herein is obtained, manufacturing efficiency will be enormously increased over present standards. Production costs will be a small fraction of what they are now. This will be the result of the worker's unrestricted productivity. By his expert knowledge and his desire for progress, he will also develop better methods and better machines for production. Because of his own natural human desire to develop his latent abilities, the worker also will develop himself greatly.

In one case well known to the author there has been a reduction in manhours per unit of production of well over 90% in the last twenty-six years. This was not the result of greater physical skill only. It was the result of the development of better machines and tools of production as well as new and better skills and designs. It was the result of the desire of all those involved in production to perfect their ideas and apply them to the production of the product.

Such a change in the attitude of workers from top to

bottom is bound to be revolutionary in its results. It is, however, an obvious step. It has been delayed because the managers of industry have largely failed in their leadership. Instead of there being management-workers leading wage-earning workers in cooperating to increase and distribute more of the goods of life to all, short-sighted managers and workers often have resisted such development. Because of its failure in leadership, management's position in the eyes of the worker also is far from what it should and must be.

Managers must regain their position as the accepted leaders of cooperating workers. The wage-payer still can boss the wage-earner, although this authority has been greatly lessened by the labor unions. Enthusiastic acceptance of the leadership of management by the worker is in most companies lacking. To regain it will take some doing.

The first step that managers must take is to get their own thinking straight. If willing cooperation is wanted, the manager must begin it and lead it. He is dealing with experts who, in most cases, are far more skillful in doing their jobs than he would be. While it is possible to boss these experts in the usual lofty way, their eager cooperation will not be won by so doing. The manager must awaken their desire to cooperate with their fellow workers in the industry, including himself. Their full cooperation cannot be obtained in any other way.

If managers are to get such desire on the part of the worker, they must review the whole program of the company seriously. A wage-earner is no more interested than a manager is in making more money for other people. His job does not depend on pleasing the stockholders, so he has no interest in dividends. Neither is he interested in increasing the efficiency of operation when such increased efficiency will result in his losing his job because management has failed to get the necessary orders. The worker is the same kind of person as the manager. He has the same needs, desires and fears. If the manager received the same treatment in all matters of income, security, advancement and dignity that he gives to the hourly worker, he would soon understand the real problem of management and have little difficulty in finding the solution.

The first question that management should answer is: What end has the company in view? What is it trying to do? In the mind of the average wage-earner today the answer is this:

"The company I work for is trying to make the largest possible profits by any method it can pursue. The profits go to absentee stockholders and top managers. They don't give a damn for the hourly workers who do the job nor for the customer who pays all costs."

With such a view, any desire to cooperate with management is unlikely. There is little reason for cooperation. The hourly worker will not go along. He sees no object in working but wages. He therefore will be uncooperative. He will be inefficient. He will be unimaginative. He will be rebellious.

The proper answer to the problem is self-evident.

Industry must make sense to the worker if it is to engage his interest. It must serve purposes that he sees and approves, if he is to cooperate eagerly in achieving them. It must have as its goal, first of all, progress, improvement in ways of living, better lives for everyone. This is, in fact, the achievement of American industry to some extent, and it should be seen clearly and adopted as the purpose of all industry. Cooperation must reward the worker in proportion to what he does. This must not be forced on management by the union, as has been true so far. It must be the program of management. Management must also protect the needs of the worker by continuous employment, as it now protects the jobs of top management.

Perhaps these goals in the light of past custom seem impossible. They are not. They are being reached now by many companies. This is a natural development.

The changing of the goal of industry from profit to service by the producing of a better and better product at a lower and lower price is what most companies claim is their goal now. It is obvious, therefore, that at least in theory, service rather than profit has become the goal. The fact is, however, that this program of service at lower prices is like our acceptance of the Sermon on the Mount; it is discussed on Sunday and forgotten on Monday. We industrialists are "practical men." We actually cannot get off the beam of profit. That is for the "eggheads." Here again we must change our ideas.

The goal of service to the customer, by giving him

71

more and more for less and less, is not only right, it is
completely practical. Where it is accepted it is far more
successful for all concerned than the policy of "all the
traffic will bear." This program is necessary if we are to
get the willing cooperation of labor. It is necessary also
if we are to get the customer's cooperating approval and
support.

Cooperation is essential to the "division of labor" that
we call modern industry. No industry can progress
without it. But there is all the difference imaginable
between the grudging, distrustful, half-forced cooperation of men who must earn wages and men greedy for
larger salaries, and the eager, whole-hearted, vigorous
and happy cooperation of men working together for a
common purpose and rejoicing in their mutual success,
their expanding industrial company.

If we are to create the atmosphere in which this willing cooperation thrives, we must change completely
the habits and conceptions that have guided management heretofore. Labor and management are properly
not warring camps; they are parts of one organization
in which they must and should cooperate fully and
happily. They are like husband and wife in this necessity. To successfully meet the competition that our
American economy now faces from abroad, we industrial managers *must* have the wage-earners' whole-
hearted cooperation.

In accomplishing this needed quality of cooperation,
management must take the lead. That is what manage-

ment is for. Its job is to lead. In doing that in the case of labor-management relations, it will be necessary to change many policies that management has followed heretofore. Management must neither exploit the customer nor the worker. Industry must continuously increase its rewards to both. Such rewards must not be forced on managers by competitors nor by labor unions. When outside force is necessary to lower costs and raise wages, management has failed in its job.

American industry has always been able to meet world competition, with its lower wages and lower material costs, whenever cooperation was achieved. Many American products now dominate the world market. All could meet world competition if cooperation such as some companies have achieved were universal.

A lower price on a better product is obtained by making such a result the desire of all the people in the whole organization. When the goal of a properly led company is better quality at a lower price, that goal will be reached. It is management's responsibility to organize or reorganize the company's program so as to accomplish just that. That is what industry is for. If it does not or cannot do that, it should disappear and eventually it will. Competition will destroy it in a free market. That is what competition is for.

Higher and higher reward should go to the worker in return for his contribution in producing the better and better product at a lower and lower cost. This progressively greater reward should go to all those in the organization, from bottom to top, depending on the contribution that each worker makes to the program of cost reduction and product improvement.

There can be no doubt that progress in industry can continue only while there is a new and growing source of buying that will absorb the products that can be made. This increased buying is done largely by the hourly worker as his income increases. If this greater income were reduced, his buying would decrease in proportion and industry to that extent would disappear. The resulting economy would be far smaller than what we now have. All industry would be affected.

In spite of the need for ever higher wages, leadership in industry has resisted every move toward giving a better income to the hourly worker. This needed buying power on which our economy is now based was forced on management by unions, not by the intelligent judgment of management.

If management had taken the lead in this matter, as it should have done, the present labor-management friction never would have developed. The workers' need for unions would not have occurred. The present war between worker and management would be impossible. The efficiency of production would be many times what we now see.

Management must rectify this error. It will be harder to do now than it would have been a generation ago. It can be done, however, and eventually must be. Many companies have done it already.

If management is to accomplish this end, it must

recognize the problem and apply the proper answer. The answer is obvious, if we will view it objectively, forgetting habit and previous custom. The worker is a man like the manager and will react to the same stimuli. He is not a man apart, in spite of the enmity that has been developed in him by the present labor-management friction. He is just as eager as any manager is to be part of a team that is properly organized and working for the advancement of our economy. However, he is not particularly struck by the idea that he has a duty toward management that management does not have toward him. He has no desire to make profits for those who do not hold up their end in production, as is true of absentee stockholders and inactive people in the company.

Management, in regaining its position of leadership, must recognize that the position of the hourly worker has changed from what it was a generation ago. He is much more powerful and also much more skilled. Manufacturing has progressed greatly. The manufacturing organization is now a group of experts who have developed new machines and methods that have almost completely eliminated the previous methods that were used. Management is not dealing with servants. It is dealing with workers of unique ability, who because of their skill are completely necessary to efficient production. It is only by cooperative use of this expert group that any manufacturing company can meet world competition or the competition in our own country.

Management cannot boss such people. It must lead

them. Managers must be accepted leaders whose leadership is respected because of ability, and whose fairness and honesty cannot be questioned. Such management must see that the abuses to which the hourly worker has been subjected by custom are eliminated. Management must see that the reward to the worker is proper and is so understood and accepted by him.

The customary abuses of lay-offs and improper use of profits are the most obvious conditions that must be changed. The reward of the worker by money and advancing position are additional ones. When the worker knows that he will be rewarded in direct proportion to this contribution and that his job is safe, his whole attitude to his work and its managers changes. He wants to increase the rewards in which he shares justly. The hourly worker does not want strikes. He does not want featherbedding. These abuses are his only means of reacting against the resistance that management has made to his progress. If managers were treated as unjustly as much management has treated wage-earners, they also would fight back, as the unions do, by any means at hand.

The abuses of labor union power are the natural reactions of human beings to the abuses to which management has subjected them. When the worker is convinced that the abuses that caused him to use such methods of reprisal no longer exist, he will join in a fair and honest program of cooperation, as he so much wants to do.

The fundamental task is to rectify the mistakes that

management has developed over the years. Labor once looked to management to lead. When management did not do so properly and fairly, the present reaction was inevitable. When management accepts its responsibility to lead in the proper way, there will be no lack of co-operation by the worker. He is a fellow player on the team and wants to be treated as such. He is not just a convenience to be used and discarded as management may decide from time to time.

The question is frequently asked: If efficiency were increased to the degree that it is in some companies and could be in all, would not the number of jobs be so small that many workers could not find employment?

The answer is obvious. Efficiency cannot eliminate jobs because increased efficiency lowers costs, lower costs cause lower prices, lower prices expand the market, and an expanding market increases employment.

Buying is controlled by price. There is no limit to human desires. Therefore, there is no limit to the market for any useful or desirable product if the price is low enough. There is no market for a product, no matter how useful, if the price is too high.

We see this fact illustrated in the number of secondhand cars that are sold, compared to new ones. If new cars were available at the price of secondhand cars, the market for new cars would expand many times. The same fact controls in the present market for ready made clothes, which is many times that of custom-made clothes, in spite of the greater attraction of clothes

77

made for the individual by a tailor. There are endless illustrations of this same fact to be seen on every hand. Cost is decisive. Cost controls the size of the market.

When the cost is reduced, as increased efficiency of cooperation reduces it, the market will be expanded indefinitely. World trade will tremendously increase. The demand for workers needed to satisfy this expanding market will constantly increase. There will be jobs without end. Prices will be falling, wages and profits rising, markets expanding, jobs increasing in number and variety, skills improving, lives will be ever richer in work and leisure and all human values.

Employment depends on the rate of buying. The rate of buying depends on price and quality. Both of these results depend on the skill and desire of the producer. The skill and desire of the producer depend on his desire for efficiency and his consequent development of his latent abilities.

There is no limit to the development of human beings and human cooperation, since man is so made by his Creator. Christ in his ministry on earth gave the world the program needed to accomplish these results. There is no mystery as to what we should do. We only need to adopt the Christian ethic.

6

How To Provide Continuous Employment

M ANY industrialists have the idea that continuous employment of hourly workers is impossible in industry. The fact that efficiency in production demands the proper solution of this problem leaves them unmoved. Habit, the result of custom, proves to their satisfaction that there is no solution. Laying off workers when business slackens has been the usual program of industrial managers. Particularly is this true of the so-called seasonal industries. Few industrialists even think of changing the custom.

The seasonal industries do have a greater problem than the manufacturers of automobiles, who customarily have a yearly shutdown during model changes.

But laying off the workers is customary in most cases where continuous employment would be far from difficult if logically considered. Lay-offs are far closer to habit than to necessity. They are often an escape mechanism for the ineffective manager.

Continuous employment is essential to industrial efficiency. The only change that is necessary for continuous employment is that management have a proper job available at all times for all employees. That is one of the responsibilities management has. Laying off the worker because of slackening of business is death to efficiency. No worker will strive for efficient production when his very efficiency will throw him out on the street that much sooner, and no sane man would expect him to do so. Naturally, he will strive to spin out the job as long as he can, by any means he can think of. Anyone else in his place would do the same thing, including the manager, who now, because of habit, follows the program of laying off when work is slack—or whenever it is more convenient for the manager than accepting responsibility would be.

A new approach must be made to this problem. The worker who is thrown out is a trained man. To replace him when the pace of industry comes back to normal will cost in most cases much more than the saving in wages that the layoff gained. That alone condemns the action. The present habit is a drain on human and industrial efficiency that must be stopped. American industry cannot afford such unnecessary losses in the

80

present world situation and the change will not be difficult if we approach the problem objectively.

Russia has solved this problem. There is no unemployment there. A job is always available to all workers, both men and women. It is obvious that if Russia solves the problem of using all human energy constantly in a dictatorship economy, we in the freer economies must solve it too, or we must admit that we are wasting human abilities that the communists are able to utilize.

Dictatorship has certain advantages. It can and often does eliminate certain failures of a free people. It would be dominant as the method of ruling nations were it not for its own weaknesses. The one most obvious is its elimination of the freedom of the individual. All progress is made by the genius of individuals. Such genius cannot be ordered. It cannot be forced. It can only be encouraged to develop.

If Edison or Kettering or our other geniuses had been in an economy dominated by a dictator they probably would not have developed the things they did since they would have been passed up by the dictatorship as unlikely men. They would not have been allowed to spend their time on their ideas. They would have been put on work given to their department by the dictatorship. Progress made through invention would be unknown to the controller of a department of a dictatorship. That is one reason why a free economy will always outdistance a dictatorship.

The solution of the problem of continuous employment is available if we will eliminate habit and think objectively. What, then, is the solution? The worker must have a guarantee from industry that if he works properly his income for proper support of his way of life will be continuous. Industry already does that for all top management and for all important producers in all parts of its operation. Industry never lays off its president, its officers, its superintendents, its recognized experts, in either office or factory. The ones laid off are the employees whom the management considers of least importance to its operation. They are usually the least able to accept the resulting lack of income. Their pay, if they were kept on, would be a small fraction of the total payroll and management should plan to have useful and profitable jobs ready for these workers under all conditions of business.

This is not a be-kind-to-the-employees plan. It is no part of management's responsibility to be merely kind to workers. Managers are responsible for efficiency in their industry. Efficiency depends on human cooperation within the industry. If genuine cooperation is to be maintained, or regained, it is absolutely essential to change the mind of the wage-earner so that his present fear of losing his income will be eliminated. That fear can be eliminated *only* by removing the danger. This can be done only by guaranteeing continuous employment.

Management must realize that continuous employment is as necessary to the manufacturing process as is proper maintenance of machines to continuous operation. Management does not sell a machine tool when it is not used during a period of slump. Management does not tear down a part of the plant because it is not used in a period of slow business. Management knows that variations in the speed of industry will always occur, as they always have.

Management must and does plan for such variations as an accepted occurrence in all departments—except that of employment. The only time management changes its operation from normal is when it lays off the hourly worker. Custom has made this action seem logical. Managers have not assessed the overall cost of taking this step compared to the cost of continuous employment. If such a comparison were made, layoffs would disappear, since the cost is far beyond the saving in any successful company.

There is not only the loss of efficient workers by such lay-offs. There is inherent in the lay-off policy, also, the much greater loss from the attitude of the employed worker toward efficiency. The cost of this attitude is many times the total pay of the man and still more disastrous in the union-enforced featherbedding that is supported by the men's fear of the layoff and its consequences. How can any wage saving by lay-off be justified in the light of these facts?

Continuous employment is the first step to efficiency. Many others follow automatically when the workers' interest in increasing efficiency is aroused, as it can be and sometimes is. How should continuous employment be given, not as a benevolence to the worker, but as a proper program of forward-looking management?

First: Manufacture to stock. The cost of such production will be less in slack times because of a continuous production schedule and the lower material costs which usually accompany such times.

Second: Develop those new machines and methods of manufacturing for more efficient production that have been indicated during the active times of operation. No company can face the future successfully without developing new equipment and methods that continuously cut costs. A slump makes available the men and the time for experimentation that would most easily accomplish such development. Plans for this development should always be on the shelf awaiting the opportunity.

Third: Reduce prices by getting lower costs. Costs can be reduced without end if we have the will and imagination to do so. In a work force of contented and sincerely co-operating men, there is an almost inexhaustible source of will and imagination serving the industry's interests. In slack times, especially, such workers are eager to help cut costs and improve methods. A slump is an excellent time to develop such a program. With the leisure, the men, and the obvious need for it, it is possible to reduce the price and make the cost justify the reduction.

Fourth: Explore the new markets that have been passed over when times were good. The foreign field is

84

an inexhaustible market. There are many markets at home also that can be developed if we will. New designs for the markets that have not been covered previously can be developed in slack times. The needs of these new markets can be explored at such times much better than when industry is active.

Fifth: Hours of work can be reduced if the worker has been informed previously and is agreeable. Such reduction of hours should be understood and agreed to by all concerned before a slump comes. This should not be done otherwise. It is well at the time of such agreement to agree also as to the maximum hours of work. Generally, the wage-earner likes to work more than forty hours per week. A fifty hour week in times of full production usually pleases him. A variation of from fifty to thirty-two hours has been a successful cushion in some cases. This cushion is much more than usually is necessary if the other plans have been properly developed.

Such a program assures the worker enough income in slack times to get by comfortably and a very good income in normal and active times. The important effect is that the worker will feel safe in helping to increase efficiency. He does not now.

Sixth: Develop new products. These are always necessary to the progress of any company. A slump will give the time, the men and the leisure to develop these products more easily than during active operation.

Progress in cost reduction takes place most rapidly in time of slump. The need for such action is pressing and the opportunity is present. Bad habits and consequent waste grow when business is at a peak. The pressures that come from slack times can be used very effectively to eliminate such wastes. This is the opportunity that a slump always gives and it should be seized.

Management should plan for slumps as a normal occurrence. Slumps have always occurred and probably always will. Slumps are useful if properly used. If they did not occur, progress would be far slower. Continuously prosperous operation is very damaging to progress, since prosperity develops wasteful habits. Slumps when planned for and properly handled can be of great help in eliminating such wastes. They should be anticipated and so used.

In planning for coming slumps, management should have the necessary assets on hand to take care of any circumstance that might happen. Lack of cash available has in some cases held up the program that should be followed. If that means fewer dividends, pay fewer dividends. Do not threaten the future of the company by reckless spending, no matter how insistent on dividends the stockholder is.

Industry is a cooperative operation. If all those who are involved want to make the company succeed, there can be no doubt of its success. When there is that feeling, prevailing slumps and booms can be and are taken in stride. Both are helpful if properly handled.

Very helpful knowledge becomes available to management during a slump. Hard times can give an accurate measure of a company's position in its field. Competitive industry is always changing. The need, attraction, price and service of any product is varying in competition with all other products. A slump often will give to management a true measure of the standing of its product that can be very valuable, even if it is at times sharply disappointing.

There is no reason why any industry cannot guarantee its employees continuous employment. It must do so if it is to be continuously successful. The attitude of the worker is final in the efficiency of production. He must be regarded as the expert he can be. He will become the expert if properly treated and led by understanding management. It is well for a manager to put himself in the place of the worker. If he does so, the needs of the situation will be clear. If he will treat the worker as he would like to be treated, his proper course will be clear and obvious to him. Here again we see the practical rightness of the Golden Rule when applied in industry. Such a course, although not traditional, is completely successful whenever adopted.

Continuous employment is a necessary program for efficiency in industry. It is necessary if we are to have full and genuine cooperation within a company. It is an obvious step if we are objective in our thinking and planning. It has not been widely accepted in industry because of habit. Nevertheless, it must be accepted if we are to get the cooperation which is so essential. Where continuous employment has been adopted, the results have been tremendous progress in efficiency. We must not let stale custom hamper that progress. We cannot do so and survive in competition with the rest of the world.

If we will follow the philosophy of Christ as given in the Sermon on the Mount, we shall have the proper answer to the problem of lay-offs. When we treat the worker as we would like to be treated, the answer is plain. Continuous employment is needed to secure the cooperation of the worker. It is also basically sound.

Management must plan to handle the problem of continuous employment by having necessary and useful work available at all times. Wages cannot properly be given to the worker in payment for work that he does not do. If we pay such unearned wages we are robbing the customer who is the only source of wages. We have no right to waste his money.

Here then is the place where a great step forward must be taken by management if we are to progress as we can and must. The rest of the world is going forward at tremendous speed. We will be outdistanced if we do not meet this competition. We must meet it and we can. That is what competition is. That is why competition is the source of most progress. It is a hard taskmaster, but its rewards are great.

7

Methods of Applying
Incentives

I NCENTIVE is usually thought of in industry as a money payment for more production. Many other incentives, far more potent than money, are available to management. Money incentive, however, is the simplest to apply and therefore is far more popular than any other type.

Money incentive is often applied as piecework. The results obtained are various and in many cases they are far from good. In other cases, piecework is at least partially successful in increasing production. It does not get to the bottom of the problem, however. Alone, it does little or nothing to create and encourage the willing cooperation of all workers in an industry.

The problem that management has in applying incentive is to make sure that the program it uses is an incentive in the mind of the worker. Does he *want* to go along? It does not follow that because managers think they are applying a good program to the workers, the workers necessarily think so too. If the plan does not inspire the individual worker to feel that he wants to do his best on the job, and keep on doing so, the incentive is far from successful. The attitude of the wage-earner absolutely determines the success of any incentive program.

What, then, are the components of a successful incentive? First, the worker must feel that he actually wants to work more efficiently and produce more. He must feel that greater efficiency will reward him in a satisfactory way. He will feel this only when his greater efficiency does in fact bring him greater rewards, both in money and in other ways as well. This has been stated before in showing how profits should be used.

The worker also must feel that greater efficiency will not in any way endanger his employment. That has been stated before in detail. Any incentive plan is useless if fear of a lay-off exists. That is still true even if the threat is imagined only in the worker's mind and does not actually exist.

The incentives that are most potent when properly offered and believed in by the worker are the following:

FIRST: Money in proportion to production.
SECOND: Status as a reward for achievement.

THIRD: Publicity of the worker's contribution in skill and imagination and the reward that is given for it. This results in added status for the worker.

The success of any incentive, as we have noted, depends completely on its acceptance by the worker. The incentive of itself will not assure results, no matter how good the managers may think it is. The worker is very suspicious of management. His experience with incentive plans has not been good. In general, managers have used incentive plans with the object of getting more production for less cost. The worker is no fool; he has seen that the object was to get him to work harder for less reward. He is apt, therefore, to be very skeptical of any incentive plan put forth by management.

It is well to keep in mind in applying any incentive system that money of itself is not as great an incentive to any of us as self-respect and status. We all will sacrifice money to keep our self-respect and to gain the respect and admiration of our contemporaries. This is shown by the enthusiasm of the amateur athlete in playing a game. The only reward he can have is self-respect and the respect of others whose good opinion he values. He will generally try harder than the professional who gets paid for his performance.

The acceptance by MacNamara of the job of Secretary of Defense, which could cost him millions, is a good example of money being passed up to gain a hoped-for status.

We see many other cases where a higher paying job

is passed up for employment that includes status but a lower salary. This can be illustrated by many people in education, the ministry and in government service. Money as a reward is far less attractive to most of us than the respect of those we know. This fact is important in the successful use of incentive plans in industry. Management has largely ignored it because many managers fail to think of a wage-earner as they think of themselves.

Status is of great importance in all human relationships. The greatest incentive that money has, usually, is that it is a symbol of success, which gives the successful man status. The resulting status is the real incentive. The ability to gain status by accomplishments which incidentally bring more income is of far greater importance to a man than the income itself. Money alone can be an incentive to the miser only.

There are certain principles that must be followed if any incentive system is to succeed. The first is that literally no limit be set on the earnings that a worker can get, except the worker's own limitations. This has to do not only with the physical skill of the operator, but most of all with his development of new ideas that may increase production far more than physical skill can. The fear that the worker often has, that if his earnings go above a certain amount the piecework price will be cut, now limits production tremendously in many plants. Glorify such ability. Stimulate it. Encourage it. Do not penalize it.

It is of course proper to change a piecework price if

management has changed the method of production so fundamentally as to justify the change. That is the only way that any change in a piecework price can be fairly made and the change must be scrupulously fair to the worker. That is the only way the worker will regard it as fair and still work with energetic good will.

There is much to be considered in this area. The worker is the expert on the job he is doing. He knows much more about it than any manager when he really wants to. If he has been properly led, and the proper incentive is offered to him, so that he actually wants to make the operation more efficient, his advice and help can be invaluable in finding better and more efficient ways to do the job. Under usual leadership he is not apt to give such help. His interest must be in the opposite direction. Here is a great opportunity for the progressive manager.

In approaching this matter of incentive in industry, it would be well to see how incentives are applied in other activities of man and the results obtained, compared to industry. We will then get a view of what proper incentive, properly applied, can realize.

The incentive that exists in all other activities of man outside of industry is almost automatic. The calling of the minister, the doctor, the lawyer or any other professional man, as well as the manager in industry, contains in itself an incentive to excel, and excellence brings rewards in self-esteem and the respect and acclaim of other men. It is only the hourly worker in industry who has no reason to try to excel. This, then, is

93

the problem that management must solve. Its solution should be relatively simple.

In industry the progress that can be made, both in the operation of the plant and in development of the worker, is usually missing. Efficiency is not developed to the degree it should be. Industry is the source of well-being, the satisfier of human necessities. Industry is of prime importance in determining the position of our country in the family of nations. Efficiency of production determines our standard of living as well as our nation's world position and influence. In spite of these facts, efficiency in industry is largely neglected. Slowdowns and featherbedding to make industry less efficient are usual with the worker and generally tolerated by management.

This is not because of the American's lack of ability compared to that of other people. When properly led, and with proper incentive, Americans can and do dominate all competition. That is to be expected, since the American is the descendant of the most progressive people of many nations. The American of today is the descendant of those who left the Old World and came to America because they wanted the freedom and the opportunity to improve themselves and their lives that they did not have in their home countries. These discontented people have made America the greatest nation that ever existed. These pioneers did not have much when they first came here. They found here little but freedom and opportunity to transform a wilderness of forests and prairies. Their industrial production, however, created such wealth that everywhere else on earth the poorest American is often regarded as a rich man. It is this possible development and its present limitations with which we must deal now.

Resistance to efficiency of production is not normal in man. It is present only when we are hired workers. We normally strive to increase our efficiency in every way we can when we play a game or when we work for ourselves. When we work for others we also do our best to work efficiently if we are in responsible positions. It is only when we are hourly workers that we resist efficiency.

Management is responsible for efficiency in industrial production. There is no doubt that the present efficiency of American production must increase or the American economy will fall behind its world competitors. Management thinks that this danger to the worker of being priced out of his job by foreign competition should make the worker do his best. In the long run management is right about the danger, but if managers look at the situation from the worker's point of view, they will reach a different conclusion.

There is no doubt that foreign competition endangers the worker's job and may in time destroy it. At present, however, the worker is far more worried about losing his job by management's failure to keep him employed in the plant where he is working. His fear of being laid off right now because of lack of orders is far more potent and also more immediate in his mind than a future danger of being priced out of his job by foreign competition. As a matter of fact, his attitude is justified.

For generations the labor unions have been indefatigable in demanding shorter hours, higher wages and better conditions for workers. By strikes and violence they have forced concessions from reluctant owners and managers. A majority of wage-earners believe that management is only greedy for profit at any cost to the workers who produce it, and that employers resist every effort to get a better life for the worker. Managers have done very little in the past to change this belief. It will take some doing now to convince the wage-earner that a manager works hard, too, and that wages are the results of their working together, so that the wage-earner will accept management as the cooperative leader of a mutual endeavor. Only managers who are totally sincere in valuing every worker as the fellow man that he is, and in wanting to cooperate with him truly and fairly, can possibly succeed in such a task.

Management would be the first to resist return to the low income of the wage-earner of a generation ago. Managers know that such reduction in the hourly worker's earnings would eliminate much of the worker's buying power and therefore eliminate much of the industry that now exists. We would have a return to the economy that was a small fraction of what we have now. The wage-earner is the main buyer of most products of industry. His prosperity is completely necessary to our successful economy. The more he prospers, the more prosperous is the whole economy, yet management has never sought enthusiastically to raise wages and keep on raising them. Management must now take a more realistic view.

If management had intelligently and willingly given the workers what the labor unions had to fight for, no labor-management friction ever could have existed. The simple human cooperation between management and men would never have been lost in the gigantic growth of American industry.

If management had been the leader of men cooperating in a mutual effort for their mutual progress in skills and prosperity, as it should have been, there would have been no reason for labor unions. A cleavage between management and labor would not exist. Efficiency of production would be many times what it is now. Foreign manufacturers could not compete in the American market as they do now. The standard of living for all would be far ahead of what we now have.

In some companies now there is harmonious cooperation between labor and management. These companies have no difficulty in meeting foreign competition. They can and do sell all over the world. The efficiency in production that comes from all men in any organization wanting to work together for a mutual purpose more than eliminates the advantage that low wages in foreign factories give to foreign industrialists. Before the present labor-management friction was introduced, American industry had no difficulty in meeting competition from starvation-wage production in other countries. American wages always have been higher than

97

wages elsewhere. Our problem now is lack of cooperation, not difference in wage rates.

Again, we see that the ethic of "do unto others as you would have them do unto you" is the practical rule that we should have followed. It is not just a Sunday-school ideal, but a proper labor-management policy.

In using money as an incentive, it is necessary first to make sure that the plan fits the conditions involved. It is a mistake to give a man something to try to induce him to be more easily led by the giver. A wage-earner is a man with the understanding and reactions of any other man. When management gives him money, with a notion of buying his loyalty, naturally he sees the motive and resents the insult. He has seen management continually resisting the union's demand for higher wages and other benefits. He will not easily believe that management has changed in character. If money is to be an incentive to sincere cooperation, it is absolutely essential that the worker earn that money. His self-respect is not developed, nor is his efficiency induced, by tips.

If money is to be used as an incentive, the program must provide that what is paid to the worker is what he has earned. The earnings of each must be in accordance with accomplishment. Only such a plan is fair to the worker and to the customer and men know what is fair and what isn't. The necessary development of competition between workers must be such that the more skillful worker's reward is in proportion to his contribution as compared to that of the less productive.

98

Everyone in the group must feel that it is a fair game and want to compete in it. If the men feel no pleasure, no fun, in the competition itself, the result of any incentive program that management may introduce will be far from what it could be. The possibilities of man, when he develops skills because of a desire to do so, are limitless, and so are the possibilities of enterprise in which men use their developing skills to increase the efficiency of the company.

The attitude of the usual worker in a union shop is to have a certain production as a limit. When he has produced so much, he stops. This may mean that the man after producing the quota he sets does nothing until the end of his shift or it may be that the speed of production is held so low that he produces no greater amount during the shift. The result is the same. It is a very small fraction of what willingly cooperating men easily produce in the same length of time.

It is obvious that no incentive plan can succeed in such plants as long as a featherbedding attitude exists. Little or no progress can be made in efficiency as long as the worker's attitude remains as it often is. A man's desire to act is his incentive to action; a man who sees nothing to gain by working more efficiently cannot be given any incentive to increase his efficiency. If the desire is lacking in the men, management cannot put incentive into them by any incentive plan. Only after management has eliminated the fears of lay-offs and rewards to the wrong people that the worker now has, with a consequent desire to limit output, can an incentive program be used to stir his desire to produce more efficiently.

The plan should reward the man not only for the number of pieces he makes, but also for all other assistance that he gives beyond his usual job. The accuracy of his work obviously adds to its value. His cooperation with management in improving methods of production is of far greater importance than any other skill. Both of these are obvious contributions he can make and he should be properly rewarded for them.

There are other ways in which his cooperation earns a reward in any successful incentive system. His attendance and his health are largely in his own control and are of great importance to the efficiency of operation. His excellence in these regards should be properly acknowledged. Of the greatest importance to progress, however, is his development. This is not only the result of being trained to do his job better. Doing his job well is of relatively small importance. The great thing is the development of his latent abilities. Given the opportunity and proper recognition of his achievements, the progress that he can make, and as a consequence the progress that his company can make because of his development, are beyond the belief of those who have not seen it.

Most industrialists find it hard to believe that such progress is available. They are therefore hesitant to try to develop it. History shows, however, that developed genius is the greatest source of progress. Progress cannot come in any other way. What we have seen so far has come from the developed potentialities of men who have become managers. Wage-earners, who because of their greater numbers have far greater potential, are largely overlooked. Here is where the coming leader will get his greatest progress. Incentive plans in general do not attempt to develop the potential powers of all the men in the plant. Management does not even recognize that possibility. That is where it overlooks its greatest opportunity.

A truly cooperative manager finds many ways to increase cooperation and reward achievement. Obviously, this cannot be done by a mechanical piecework plan only. There should be an overall bonus based on the contribution each person makes in any way that is helpful to overall efficiency. If each person is properly rated on all these things and paid accordingly, there will not only be a fair reward to each worker, but much more important, there will be friendly and exciting competition between the workers, so that each tries to outdistance the others and to contribute more. A spirit of teamwork will prevail, as it does between competing members of a football team. The results will seem miraculous when compared to the results of the usual cut-and-dried policy now followed.

Money incentive has been stressed, since it is used in almost all cases. If it is to be most effective, however, it must be combined with status and publicity. Promotion of the people in any company must be determined by their record made in production, both in skill and imagination. The worker must feel that higher status is a natural reward for achievement (as of course it should be) and management must make sure that outstanding achievement is fully recognized, is known throughout the plant, and receives promotion. When money, status and publicity are used accurately and honestly by scrupulously just leadership, they are incentives that completely capture the worker's imagination. He will not only be a cooperating operator, he will also be a rapidly developing individual, with rapidly increasing ability. This is how efficient industrial organizations are built.

In following out this program, we must act on the principles that Christ taught to the world in his ministry here. The basis of this program is human fellowship, based on the brotherhood of man. This kind of quality is a practical fact; each one of us is a unique person, but we are all equally human. Here is a principle of human nature as real as any principle of physics. It becomes as obvious as the law of gravitation, when we break away from the habit of thinking of labor and management as different things.

Eventually this spirit of brotherhood should prevail in all industry. Where they prevail now, there is a revolution in production and progress. Men find new ways of saving time and materials and increasing efficiency, production is many times greater—especially in shops where labor-management friction existed. Costs are reduced, and prices cut, but profits, wages and bonuses are greatly expanded. Men who are accomplishing such results are revealing obvious roads to a future progress that will make past and present accomplishments seem picayune.

These United States of America are founded on the principle that all men are born equally endowed by our Creator with certain rights. We have reversed the field in recent years. We cannot do otherwise than change what we are now doing in labor-management relations, or we will disappear as a dominant nation.

The answer is obvious if we will be objective and forget past habit. The threat we face is frightening. We must answer it, and soon.

America is a nation of many men who came here from all parts of the earth. Until a generation ago, Americans had gone farther in human progress and in health, happiness and shared prosperity than any other people. In recent years we have reversed that course. We must get back to basic Christian and American principles again. We must resume the forward surge toward a new and better future, or America will disappear as the leader of the new world.

8

Industry and Taxation

G OVERNMENT is completely necessary to any economy. But it can be—and has been—completely ruinous to progress. While government is necessary in attaining progress, too much government completely eliminates freedom and reverses human progress. Government is like food. In proper amounts and proper character it is necessary to life and growth. In too great quantity and in wrong quality it is completely destructive. Government, like gluttony, grows on people as a habit, if not restrained.

No citizen at first can believe that his own government can be anything but helpful, after seeing how necessary it is. When its destructive dominance does become evident, however, the citizen, like the glutton, because of developed weakness, will seldom take the necessary steps to eliminate its dangers. The decline and fall of all nations has followed an increase in the power of government over its subjects.

The dominance of government is usually desired by weak people. They want their government to do the things that they are too lazy or too weak to do for themselves. No virile people would ever allow government, either their own or any other, to dominate them, as all history attests. When people soften to the extent that they cannot rely on themselves, they go to government for help. What actually happens then is this: government helps them with what it takes *from* them. (They are the government's only source of income; government *produces* nothing.) Being helped, instead of helping themselves, they produce less. Government, to support them, must take a larger part of their production. Finally, they can no longer support the government's take. Then, either a new, still stronger, government smashes their weaker government in war (as Rome did Egypt) or the government simply collapses when its subjects can't support it (as Rome eventually did). Government ultimately destroys itself.

What, then, are the proper functions of government? The primary reason for its existence is to protect the freedom of its people. In so doing, it must limit the actions of its citizens to some extent. Only so can other freedoms that are more important be protected. As an illustration, government must limit the freedom of the

106

automobile driver so that he does not become a danger to other drivers. There are other restrictions necessary to the freedom of all that must be imposed on some. Such restrictions are obvious and must be continuously made by government to maintain individual freedom. They do not restrict basic freedom, but do just the opposite.

The restrictions that we are dealing with in large government, those which eliminate our freedom, have to do with forcing the citizen to use his time and efforts to support governmental activities that do not promote his progress, such as governmental infringing on the rights of all to promote the well-being of a minority.

The freedom that was present in the government developed by our founding fathers has now been changed greatly. Many of the protections that they put into our Constitution have been eliminated by amendment and by Supreme Court interpretations. Many of the difficulties we find ourselves in are the result of these changes.

When government grows beyond the servant stage, its attitude toward the citizen changes. It no longer is a helper. It changes to a controller. There is no doubt that those in authority can make a good case for their control being for the purpose of meeting a crisis. It is by this device that government usually is given the power that it must have to dominate. The powers given to government by the voters at the time of crisis to overcome real or fancied difficulty are then made permanent. Control is taken from the people. The present rôle of the Pentagon is an obvious example. War preparation was accepted as necessary by the citizenry during the last war. It has become permanent now.

Taxation for the support of our government may be excessive, but it is necessary if government is to do the things that the war program and social security demand. Such taxation has been made possible only by changing our Constitution from what it was as originally written by our forebears. Only by changing it to permit an income tax at steeply punitive rates (which Karl Marx first prescribed as a certain method of wrecking a free society) could our present dominant government be developed.

No matter how government grows, no matter how reasonable its growth seems at first, large government spells death to freedom and eventual suicide for that very government, as all history proves. Freedom and dominant government cannot exist together.

In our own government we see an illustration of this. Near the beginning of the century we wanted government to assume more responsibility for individual lives. Because of this, the income tax was initiated. This tax was contrary to the Constitution. The founding fathers saw that growth of government through taxation threatened freedom and they gave the federal government no power to tax except in payment for services to those taxed and in proportion to the service. To eliminate this safeguard, the Constitution had to be amended. The proposed income tax was so small at first that few saw any danger in the amendment and its opponents had little support. When the income tax *principle* was accepted, however, the present abuses were assured.

It is noteworthy that the present punitive tax could be imposed only by degrees. There would have been a revolution if the present taxes that have grown from the first entering wedge had been collected at the outset. In fact, when a congressman predicted during the debate on the income tax amendment that the tax would grow until it took ten percent of some incomes, he was bowled over by the statement that if such unfairness should be attempted there would be a revolution. We have now come to a point where income taxes take more than 91% of every successful manufacturer's income. This confiscation had to be done slowly, however, by fighting wars that were called wars for survival. The increased tax was accepted then for that reason. It was not difficult to continue it after we had become inured to it. There is little doubt that it will be continued during the so called "Cold War."

Such a tax program has many destructive effects, but the one germane to our subject is its effect on the operation of industry. The incentives that stimulated the growth of industry up to a generation ago have been largely eliminated in recent years. Profit in industry, which originally was the reward to the owner, is now largely taken by government in taxes. Today, no industrialist can get any great reward from owning and operating an industry, no matter how successful it may be. The only way the owner can get any fair reward

109

for having created an industry is to sell it out. He then has to pay the government only 25% of its value and is then taxed less than half as much as before. If he continues to work to expand his industry, thereby increasing employment and raising the general standard of living, he gets little for his labor. He must first of all pay 52% of the industry's profits in taxes and then his personal income tax, on any money he gets, up to 91%. There is no way that he can win. He will, however, lose less by selling out and quitting work, which is happening now.

This policy, which Government forces on industrialists, has changed the operation of industry. Up to a generation ago, American industry in general was operated by founders and owners. Now it is largely run by hired managers of combined companies. The genius who was responsible for the creation and growth of the company has sold out and quit. The result is that industrial policy has changed from energetic development of an industry to getting maximum profits for the stockholder. The new management is hired for that purpose. No other policy is attractive to the new owners. Profit is their only reason for buying the business from the founder and combining it with their other holdings. There is no doubt that such large organizations have the ability to make large profits. These could be the result of efficient operation, but they are usually the result of controlling the market in order to stabilize prices. Competition is held in check.

There is little doubt that cooperation between labor

and management is less than it was under private ownership. There is also little doubt that the progress in development of new products is less than it was and still would be under private ownership. However, the profit of such industry has increased by this concentration. The increase does not come from more efficient production. This is shown by the rapid price increases. There is little doubt that overall efficiency of production has decreased.

The reason generally given for the rising costs of such organization is increased wages. Doubtless these have some effect, but they need not be a controlling reason. Individually controlled companies have absorbed these wage increases and the higher prices of the raw materials they must buy and nevertheless have lowered costs and selling prices.

The greatest reason for higher costs in these multi-unit companies is the friction developed between labor and management in the new environment, and the changing of management's goal from progress to profit. The workers from top to bottom are not anxious to make more profit for absentee owners who feel no responsibility for the industry and neither know nor care about them. They work without enthusiasm or much interest, for nothing but wages and salaries.

But the greatest failure that results from this new direction of industry is the neglect of the customer's interests. The new program is not pointed to give the customer more and more for less and less, as was generally the case when active competition kept the wholly

111

owned smaller units briskly bidding for more customers.

The eventual outcome of this governmental policy of punitive taxation of the successful industrialist is in the future. The first results are shown in the friction between labor and management and its lowering of the efficiency of operation, with resulting high costs of production. The worker is not enthusiastic about the new policy. He does not believe in rewarding the stockholder instead of the producer and the customer.

The result of the change is evident also in the relative lack of progress that industry is making in America compared to that made in other parts of the world. We are told that we are pricing ourselves out of the world market. That is true. The reason usually given is high wages here compared to the rest of the world. That is not the reason, since industry that has obtained cooperation from its workers can pay much higher wages and still sell its products all over the world.

America is losing out in competition with industry in the rest of the world because the necessary leadership here is punished for its success. No industrialist will develop an industry in an atmosphere of penalty for success. The unequal taxation inflicted on industry is not only unfair on the basis of reward, but it also makes the industrialist of genius feel that success is not wanted because of the laws that penalize it.

If American industry is to meet world competition, we must change our taxation program. Government cannot be permitted to continue its punishment of successful industrial operation. The existence of government itself depends upon a healthy economy. Government produces nothing. Productive men must support it. Our government's insane policy of discouraging and penalizing its most productive supporters must eventually cause that government's collapse.

It is necessity to develop the genius that is in the American people. The record shows that when men are free to develop their potential abilities, they accomplish feats that seemed impossible before. Countless Americans, such as Bell, Edison, Carnegie and Ford, have shown that an industrial genius, having freedom, can beat the world in progress, quality and cost. Such genius is our hope in the future. We must welcome its appearance. We must encourage it with proper rewards. It must not be punished. We must see to it that such men keep the rewards that naturally come to them in return for their great services to all of us. When that is done, the leader who has created a new company and developed its products will not sell out and quit as he does now. He will continue in industry. He will build the little enterprise into a great new industry. The industrial genius now latent and discouraged will then go on raising our standard of living to heights now unimaginable, as American genius did up to the present time.

9

How Profits Should be Used

THE place in which much new thinking must be done is in the proper distribution of the profits of industry. It is obvious that all profits come from the customer when he buys the manufactured product. How much should he be charged? The price must cover all the costs, plus a profit. What is to be the price and what is to be the profit? This is the most important policy decision that management must make: "What is to be the price, and how do we make it the proper one? How do we determine what that price should be?"

The present methods of pricing the products of industry do not in most cases consider sufficiently all the factors that should be weighed. For example, we do not usually consider the responsibility that an industry owes to the economy. We are apt to think that our own industry is solely for the purpose of giving a profit to its owners. We do not realize that there are responsibilities that go far beyond if we consider all factors. All industry is dependent on the whole economy. To think of it in terms of an individual or a company activity is bound to lead management in wrong directions. It will result in a company that is far from a fully successful operation.

All industry is completely dependent upon the general economy. If the rest of the economy were removed no one industry could exist. Its livelihood and its existence depend wholly on being part of a team. Successful management must accept their public responsibility. If they do not, the usefulness of the company and its success will be far from what it could be.

There are many facets of this responsibility. The one being discussed here is the proper use of the profits that industry makes. As has been shown, government by its tax program now takes a great part of all profits. These taxes cannot be paid by the industry; they are passed on to the customer. Industry must finish up with the same profit after the government's take. It is not possible for industry to exist otherwise.

While it is true that the profit tax is paid by the customer, the result to the owner and the whole economy is very serious. Since in the case of a privately owned industry most of the profit that industry makes is taken by government, pricing for a proper profit is impossible in an economy where the speed of industry varies widely as it does in America. Pricing is difficult when each dollar of gross profit is taxed differently. If the profit is used as retained earnings the tax is fifty-two percent. If it is used as a reward to the worker or owner it is taxed up to or over ninety-five percent.

If we are to properly reward the people who produce the product and who reduce the price by their skill and cooperation, no management can price the product accurately. The price would have to be changed as the speed of the industry changed. Cost varies widely as volume of production changes. Is there any wonder that some things are priced at more than ten times the cost of production, while other products cannot be made at a profit at all by many companies? Competition is a hard taskmaster in many cases, but sometimes it does not appear at all when prices are controlled.

If management sells at a price that is determined by competition, whatever reward is given to any one of the three interested parties—labor, customer or stockholder—must be taken from the others. If wages are increased, with no change in efficiency, the price must be increased or the stockholder must get less. If, however, efficiency of production is sufficiently increased by any means, be it better tools, better design, better materials or greater efficiency on the part of the worker, then the reward can be increased, depending on the judgment of management, without increasing price.

It is obvious that the customer's interests should be the first goal of industry. He pays all costs, taxes and profits. He is completely necessary to any and all industry. Pleasing him must be the program of industry. In doing that, the most important person from a cost standpoint is the worker. He alone can make the product of a quality and at a price that will please that customer. He must be rewarded for this and rewarded in proportion as he accomplishes the purpose. The worker includes all people who design and produce the product from top to bottom.

The last person who is involved in production is the stockholder. His contribution is usually very questionable. By "stockholder" in this connection, it is not meant to include the founder of a company or those who first helped him to buy his tools. Such stockholders usually are workers, as the term is used here. The stockholder we are discussing now is the investor who buys stocks of companies as an investment. Such stockholders have no interest in the company other than dividends and an increased stock price. They contribute nothing to the efficiency of the company and have little or no knowledge of its operations.

The theory on which such stockholders are rewarded is that they supply the money for the needs of the company. This is true to a very limited extent. If we will review the methods that are usually followed by manufacturing companies who expand their operation and must have money to do it, we will see that almost all of the money that is so used by them comes from retained earnings or bonds. Of course, bonds serve the same purpose as retained earnings. They merely delay the time at which the earnings are retained. The only exceptions to this program are the publicly controlled companies such as telephone, power and light and other public utilities. They of course want to increase their shares of stock since the charges that they can make for their services is determined by the profit they can make on the investment. The more stock they have the more profit they can collect from the public.

The usual stockholder who buys stock on the exchange would never think of putting money into a company at the time it is most needed. Such organizations at the start get their money from the founder and perhaps from his friends who go into the business with the founder.

The stockholder considered here is the one who buys stock only after the company has achieved success. He will buy stock then, because he believes it will increase in price and dividends more than any other stock he could buy. He has no other interest or purpose.

When any company has achieved success so that it is attractive as an investment, all money usually needed for expansion is supplied by the customer in retained earnings. It is obvious, therefore, that the customer's interests, not the stockholder's, should come first. The founders who stay with the company in executive capacities usually get their greatest reward in salary, as do all other workers in the operation.

It is of course true that this program is far different from what is now customary. The program outlined for labor-management cooperation also is far different from what is now customary. If progress is to be made, it can be done only by changing the present custom. The changes outlined in properly rewarding the proper people have proved to be very successful where used. All three segments—customer, worker and even absentee stockholder—have been far better rewarded in such operations than is now usual in companies with labor-management friction. The program of proper reward of the proper people has proven itself by long experience.

There must be a review of our thinking about profits in industry. We must change our goal from "all the traffic will bear" to "a better product at a lower price." This must be done in spite of the problems that the present taxation program inserts into the picture. The philosophy of Christ will guide us properly in spite of the difficulties that government and custom have put into the problem. The right answer is obvious if we will think it through.

The program now usual in industry is bound to fail since it is wrong. It will court competition from other countries as it is now doing. It will develop more and more friction with the worker. It will develop higher and higher prices that will eventually price the selfishly operated company out of the market.

We can, by government action on tariffs and by controlled prices, overcome the difficulty of foreign and domestic competition to some extent. Tariffs, however, destroy all markets abroad and also tend to restrict the market at home because of the higher prices that they encourage. Tariffs are not the answer and never can be. Americans must rise to the occasion. We have done it before and can do it again. We must increase efficiency of production and by so doing lower costs and prices.

We are very apt to excuse our present lack of efficiency by claiming that foreign labor is much cheaper than labor here. We claim that we are defeated by this difference in wage rates. This same difference has always existed. It is only recently that we have been losing our place competitively. Since we met foreign competition before, we can now if we will rise to the challenge. The worker in other countries has always been paid less than the American worker. That is the main reason why he came here as an immigrant. It is only recently that we have failed to meet foreign competition. We can and must meet it now.

The American industrial leader heretofore has been able to accept the wage differential and still win in competition with his foreign competitors because of his ability and the excellence of the worker who originally came here from Europe because he was dissatisfied with the conditions in his own country. Such men are more developed than those content to stay in Europe. They can beat the ones who remained and always have. It was the American industrialist's genius for leadership of outstanding workers which made this possible. He has now failed to get the cooperation of the worker and is losing out because of friction. When he gets cooperation, he can and will win again. This is not a theory only, it is the history of all manufacturers who have designed a proper product and built it with cooperative workers. Wage rates per hour are of little importance in themselves. The important feature is wage cost per piece. This depends on efficiency of operation and on that only.

When a properly designed product is made by cooperative workers the cost can be reduced by any amount desired by the group involved. When the worker is rewarded and stimulated by what he does in a way acceptable to him, such cooperation can be gained. Most of the problems that face industry, such as strikes, featherbedding, foreign competition and high costs, disappear. This is always true when a proper philosophy is followed by dedicated people. That is our only problem now in making American industry completely successful.

The distribution of profits comes second to making them. If the efficiency of industry is high enough, the problem of how to distribute the profit becomes to some extent secondary, since all those who accomplish the purpose will be rewarded by the policy that produced the efficiency. The price and cost are already reduced by the policy of cooperation which in turn rewards the customer. The worker will be rewarded properly, since he must be if he is to cooperate. The absentee stockholder also will get his share, even if undeserved, out of the greatly increased profit that the efficiency produces.

There is no other known way that America can meet

the problems that we now face from foreign competition and foreign progress. If we Americans will accept the challenge as did our forefathers, the future is assured. We only need to accept our responsibility to the economy.

10

Product Program in the Operation of Industry

THE question can well be asked, What should a manufacturing company produce? This question is answered accurately when a successful company starts, since the purpose of starting it is to produce an article that is expected to be better, all things considered, than anything else of its kind on the market. After some success has been obtained, there is often the desire to grow to greater size and importance. The management then often decides to produce other products or buy other companies, the need for which is doubtful. At that time, the desire is often for larger size rather than for more or better service to the public. This is a wrong direction to take.

The first point in any successful manufacturing program is that the interests of the customer should be controlling. If management does not plan to offer the customer something better and/or cheaper than all competing manufacturers offer, the firm can contribute nothing and should not go into the field. It would be useless in it. The manufacturer is in competition with all other producers in the same way that a professional baseball player is in competition with all other ball players. If he cannot contribute more to the success of his team than anyone else available, he is out. The spectators and even the players themselves want it that way. Ability is then recognized and rewarded in relation to excellence.

The excellence that the successful producer has may be widely varying. It is perhaps impossible for any manufacturer to be better in all regards than all of his competitors. But he should and must excel all competition in some way if he is to be successful. His product can be more efficiently made and be cheaper in price. It may be designed for different uses. Or it may be applied to the customer's needs in a way that will make it more useful because of the application. It may be more economically distributed. There are countless ways in which the product can be made more attractive to the customer. If this is done, then there is a place in the economy for the company that does it. The important point is that no one should go into the production of any product unless he can help the user be better off than he would be if the producer were not in the field. The consumer's interests are paramount. The producer can succeed only when he gives the consumer some benefit or satisfaction that no one else does.

In organizing for efficiency that will meet competition, the abilities that are available to management should be followed. There are three branches of a manufacturing company. The first is engineering. The second is production. The third is distribution. No company has been dominant in all three activities.

Management should organize its operations according to the abilities available in each of these branches. If it is best in engineering, the excellence of the product and its development should be the area that should be followed primarily, the expectation being that such development will outdistance competition.

If production is the company's strongest area, manufacturing methods and costs should be the foundation on which success is based. The cost of the product and its continuing reduction will be the key to success.

If distribution is the strongest area, selling can be made the foundation of success in competition. The product, its cost and its distribution are all related, but the available abilities vary.

The direction and development of growth will differ when management lets policy follow the line of greatest opportunity dependent on the abilities available.

If engineering is to be dominant, then a better product, better designed, must be made.

If efficient production is to be the foundation of success, then fewer products should be made so that cost reductions can be more rapidly accomplished.

If efficient distribution is to be the basis on which management plans for success, then service, and proper application of the right product can be made of great benefit to the customer.

The operation of a company may be vastly different because of the abilities available. Just as in a game of football, the program that is followed will depend on the abilities available and the skills of the players, in comparison with the competition. In the same way, the program that is followed by competing companies who succeed may be widely different and usually is.

A decision on how best to operate is the first and very important one for the manager to reach. The next step is to make continual progress in the development of the program adopted. In accomplishing this, the primary need is for the thinking of those who are responsible for progress to be in the right direction. The first step is acceptance of the fact that everything now done is wrong compared with the better way in which it can and eventually will be done. This is an obvious fact, but it is not accepted generally, in spite of its truth. History shows that every design can be bettered, every method can be improved, every material can be replaced by a better and/or cheaper one. The difficulty is that our minds are so dulled by habit that often they do not recognize and accept a new and better idea soon enough. The job of the leader is to see that the workers' minds are alert and that they desire to develop every possibility of progress.

When we accept the obvious fact that everything we do can be done better, and operate accordingly in our thinking and acting, progress in cost, economy and improvement will be continuous. Such continuous progress is the responsibility of the manufacturer to the consumer.

The industrialist must be the expert in his line if he is to be successful. When he is the expert, he will lead the customer in the direction he should go for the best interests of the customer. If he can't lead the customer in the direction he should go, he is of no value and should get out.

The obvious illustration of the failure of management in directing progress is the automobile. There is much experience with it, since it is a universal tool in America. Automobile management decided that yearly change and unusual appearance would increase sales and profits. Because of this decision, tremendously expensive annual redesigns have made the usual car that is now offered to the public more than twice as costly as it would have been with a standard design that would be without these fillips.

The decision was not that of the expert who accepts his responsibility to the customer. It was wrong, as experience has shown. The customers needed a smaller, cheaper, more efficient, more easily maintained car. The manufacturer, however, wanted to make each year's car obsolete the following year. If a good standard car at a very much lower cost had been made, the automobile industry would have been of far greater service. It also would be more prosperous, since foreign competition would not have come into the market.

We see here the benighted attitude of the automobile industry toward the customer. Instead of following the Golden Rule, those responsible for the industry's direction followed the philosophy that is common in industry, of trying to exploit rather than to serve the customer. It was the industry's hope that it could inflate the customer's vanity, stimulate his envy, make thrift seem shameful and overcome prudence so that he would go in debt to buy a new car every year, since the design and appearance were changed that often. It did not succeed. Instead, it made the competition of the foreign cars tremendously greater, so that a significant part of the market was taken over by them.

It is strange that industrialists forget the example of Henry Ford the first. He gave to the customer an excellent standardized car at a continually lower price. His price for the same car went from nearly a thousand dollars to less than three hundred dollars in twenty years. He also rewarded the worker at more than the going rate. And he was financially successful. He was, as a matter of fact, much more successful financially than any man has been since. We see here again the illustration of the soundness of the Christian ethic. All who act according to it succeed. A far different result from treating fellow men as victims to be preyed upon.

Another program of industry has an important effect

on its success. There has been in recent years a growing tendency to buy out other companies, so that the purchasing company increases in size and multiplies the number of its products. That purchase may also reduce competition or it may secure some desired personnel. To a large extent this practice is part of the distortion of the economy caused by the present exorbitant taxes.

Often, the purchased company has had a loss in the previous years' operations and the present regulations are so insane that such a loss becomes an asset. The purchasing company buys the unprofitable company frankly for "tax loss" which can be used as a deduction to reduce the new owner's tax. In other cases, a disheartened owner sells out and quits, at a cost of only the 25% capital gains tax, rather than struggle on to expand a company burdened with an annual profit tax of 52%, plus the usual added income taxes.

In the final analysis, the success of this policy is doubtful. The result depends greatly on how the purchase affects the buying company's objectives. It introduces many new problems into the company's operation. The most obvious one is that the management has more things to produce and more personnel to manage. This makes leadership more difficult. As any organization becomes more complicated, its efficiency obviously is reduced. No manager can be as expert in two things as he can be in one. Success of any organization depends on its relative efficiency compared to competing organizations. As size and complications increase, efficiency tends to decrease. This does not mean that better management and better organization will not beat the less able. It does mean that any ability of leadership will decrease in efficiency as the complications increase. The large multiple company will fall behind more simple and compact competitors—if competition controls price.

The future of any company depends on its success in serving the customer. The better this is done, the greater the success. The expert will always do this better with one or a few products than with many. His chance for success depends on his doing a few things well, rather than many things not so well.

What, then, should be the direction of a company's growth? The basic consideration is service to the consumer. The management must always hold the advantage over competitors of being able to give the customer something better in some way than competition can offer. Since increasing a company's size and multiplying its products usually will not increase that advantage, it should not be done.

The industrialist, since he is and must be the expert in his line, must be able to see the direction that progress should take in that line. He must be able to produce and sell the things the customer should have in an advancing economy. The customer may resist at first, but the industrialist must show him the direction he should go and why. That is the industrialist's responsibility.

There is no doubt that it is often easier to accept the wrong ideas that the customer may have. If they are not right, it is the responsibility of the industrialist to lead the customer in the way he should go even when the customer resents it. He must have the expert knowledge and ability to do this in spite of resistance.

Making one product constantly better and cheaper is relatively easy compared to doing the same thing to many products. It is well, also, to recognize that there is no limit to the market for any useful product if the product is good enough and cheap enough.

It is generally supposed that there is a limit to any cost reduction that can be made. It is doubtful that this is true. There is little doubt, if an automobile company were operated today by Henry Ford the first as he was in his prime, that we would be buying automobiles at less than a third of the present prices. The changes on the cars' design also would be made for utility, not prestige. The price would go continually down.

In the final analysis the interests of all people are the same. When we believe that if we take advantage of someone we will gain by so doing we are completely wrong. All wrongly selfish acts eventually harm the perpetrator as well as the victim. Exorbitant prices can be thought of as gain to the one who gets them, but in the final analysis such pricing will destroy the market for the product and wreck the seller. He would eventually be far more successful if he had charged the right price.

It is the interdependence of all people on earth that makes the Christian ethic necessary. Christ's teaching is completely practical. And it is eventually completely necessary if we on earth are even to survive. It answers all the problems that man has. Eventually it must be the plan of life for all people who remain on earth. If we do not follow it we shall perish as our power of destruction grows.

When we do operate on the principles that Christ announced—

We shall have cooperation between labor and management.
We shall have no inflation.
We shall have our trade rapidly expanding with all countries.
We shall eliminate most taxation.
We shall eliminate war and preparation for it.
We shall have a tremendously higher standard of living.
We shall have much more able people.
We shall be much more content.

11

Economic Waste

THERE has been much discussion about waste incurred in the free enterprise system and what should be done about it. There are laws to stop the wasteful destruction of our forests and other natural resources. One of the many arguments advanced for socialism is that it would stop waste, the assumption being that bureaucrats are more thrifty than free enterprise operators. It is strange that people suppose that men are more careful of other men's property than of their own. In fact, government operation always has been far more wasteful than private enterprise.

The waste of materials in industry, however, is negligible compared to management's waste of the abilities of the hourly worker. Few managers give serious attention to the development of a man, particularly of a wage earner who does manual work. The college graduate is much sought after and put into work that is intended to stimulate and develop his abilities. The hourly worker is rarely given the opportunity and the challenge that will develop his. He is not usually considered as a prospect for development.

It is of course true that the educated man often has developed more than the usual hourly worker. This, however, is far from conclusive as to his future possibilities. There are many people with relatively little education who, because of their greater effort, sparked by their handicap of lack of education, will develop farther than the educated man who feels that he has at least partially arrived.

Genius is not the result of education. Edison was not a Ph.D., nor was Kettering. Latent talents and abilities are present in every normal child. These grow as the individual's effort to develop them increases. This development is usually the result of individual desire, not of formal education. Although some people have more native or latent ability than others, everyone has great innate powers that he can develop. Everyone can become more than he is now. This is as true of mental ability as it is of physical ability.

Perhaps we can compare those changes in a man called development of latent abilities with what takes place when the temperature of water changes. Whether water is ice, liquid or steam depends on how much heat is applied. These forms of water are not similar. Their appearance, usefulness and actions are entirely different. They remain, however, water. The change that takes place in coal is another illustration. Coal was once plant life. By pressure and temperature it was changed to coal. By union with the oxygen in the air it burns and produces heat. If it remains inert in the form of coal it has little utility. Here it parallels the relative uselessness of an undeveloped man. A change in the environment permits water and coal, and also men, to change themselves and develop latent powers of usefulness.

A man can by development of his latent abilities become a person of great usefulness. Freedom and a challenging environment can spark the ambition needed to develop his abilities. These developments make as much difference in a man's usefulness as do the changes that heat makes in water or coal. The one difference in this simile is that there are fixed limitations to what water and coal can become. The possibilities of man through development are almost limitless.

Perhaps no two people are alike. Perhaps there are latent abilities in some people that do not exist in others. Nevertheless, no one yet has fully developed all his latent abilities. There may be limitations to an individual's possible development, but no one yet has ever reached such limitations. That certain abilities may exist in only a few persons does not change this fact. The waste of the potential in all of us is enormous and tragic. It is this waste with which we must deal.

Men have an endless variety of abilities. Individual freedom called forth a development of human abilities that no one had ever imagined before and these developed abilities created the industrial revolution. These abilities are still developing. We live today in a world undreamed of only decades ago and tomorrow we will live in a universe unknown now. Since development by man is limitless, its directions, as we are seeing, are almost infinite.

As men develop themselves, they develop new needs and desires, and to satisfy these, they develop new industry and science and new directions for them to take. Man will develop in the future new abilities of which he is now not conscious. The need for these abilities does not now exist. As men change the world, they develop a need for new abilities and skills and the reason to direct their uses to new ends. Men change themselves as they change their environment and the new environment produces new incentives for them.

The changes in our lives that have resulted from man's self-development were unbelievable a century ago. No one a hundred years ago could imagine any of the things that are commonplace now—television, air travel, radio, electric lights and telephone. Nor can we imagine now what man's development will give to future generations.

Tremendous as has been this progress in the last hundred years, it has been the result of the genius of a very few people. Only a few developed to the extent that they made possible the progress we have seen. If we had given freedom and incentive to all people, so that they might have developed themselves, the progress that would have occurred would have been enormously greater. There are many latent geniuses. We do not now recognize them any more than we recognized the possibility of a Kettering or an Einstein a century ago.

We have never equalled the painting of the Italian Renaissance or the music produced in Germany in the 18th and 19th centuries. Our incentives are now in other directions. If the major incentives were again in the direction of art and music, we should now be developing in those directions. We should not have the silly blots that undeveloped artists call "modern" art. In these futile attempts, however, we see the universal aspirations of mankind. Man always wants to excel and be outstanding in some way. He is not content otherwise. The undeveloped people who attempt such art or music must know that they have not developed their artistic abilities. They have not tried hard enough or long enough to develop them. In order to claim the reputation that they desire they attempt to set up new standards, since they cannot in their undeveloped state compete with past genius.

We see the same incentive in the struggle of the athlete to break previous records. The same desire is present in people who attempt by dress and habit to outshine others, thin as such accomplishment is. This desire to excel is an incentive in all people. The resulting development depends on the competition and how they meet it.

139

We have in Japan an outstanding example of development of abilities because of incentives resulting from economic pressures. Japan has a population of over 90 million people who live in an area less than that of the State of Montana. Most of this area is not arable land. It contains very few natural resources. Nevertheless, the Japanese have produced a successful economy. They are now so efficient in producing some things that the United States must raise tariff barriers that exclude their manufactured products, since Americans cannot compete with them.

Because of his imperative needs and his environment, the Japanese has developed himself to a point where he makes his economy outstanding in spite of every natural handicap. If 90 million outsiders were suddenly put into Japan and forced to stay there, they would starve, because they wouldn't have developed the ability to overcome the environmental difficulties. They would not have developed in the directions necessary, as have the Japanese. There is no evidence of any fundamental superiority of the Japanese over other people. They are one of many illustrations of the development of man under pressure of necessity to a point where he excels others who developed less because of lack of economic pressure.

If the pressure caused by necessity or by other strong incentives were present, all persons would develop to the extent necessary to live the kind of life they want. It is only the lack of such spurs that lets man's abilities lie dormant. When the incentive is there, the man increases his ability. If the spur is not there, he follows routine habit. Such people remain static.

Why are we content to let ourselves be only a shadow of what we could be? Why don't we develop our latent abilities to the utmost, as we can? The first reason is that we are apt to underrate ourselves. We doubt that we can develop far beyond what we are now. We do not believe in ourselves, so we fail to rise to the heights to which we are capable.

The second reason for our failure to develop as we can is our lack of desire. We are getting along all right; why try harder?

The third reason is habit. Those with whom we associate perhaps do not try to develop. We do not want to be different or thought peculiar.

These attitudes, which are all too common, are also encouraged by our governmental policy of supporting anyone who does not exert himself. Consequently, many people accept this easier way of living. They do not need to—and soon will be unable to—develop themselves. They remain static and eventually become helpless.

The industrialist's failure to put incentives into the plant environment of the wage earner also encourages this inertness. The wage earner feels, and in most cases rightly so, that he does not control his future. No matter how well he does his work, his increased ability makes no difference. He will still be dropped off the job whenever work gets slack. If he advances in pay or status, he does so through favoritism or luck, not by his own efforts. Hence, he has little incentive to develop; therefore in most cases he does not. It is unusual for the wage earner to take any other attitude and perhaps he should not with our present industrial customs.

There are, however, some people who feel within themselves an overwhelming challenge to develop, even when their environment offers no incentive or visible reward to be gained. Such men develop themselves and rise to the top. To them, the obstacles that our present industrial customs present become an incentive, since even greater effort is required to surmount them. An example of such exceptional development is the American Negro. He is handicapped in opportunity by our present beliefs and customs. To succeed he must try harder and develop further than his white brother. The result is that in one century, millions of Negroes have done much in self-development. The grandchildren of slaves are now cultured men and women, artists, musicians, bankers, journalists, whose contributions to American life are outstanding. George Washington Carver was an important scientist. Booker Washington was an outstanding educator. Marian Anderson is a great singer and Dorothy Dandridge is a great actress. The Negro is also supreme in all forms of athletics. His development is the result of outstanding effort, sparked by handicaps.

As our environment changes, our needs change. Because of this, our incentives change in direction. Generations ago, man had to walk, dig and carry, and to combat wild animals. He therefore developed certain abilities. The need for such powers has largely disappeared now, as our knowledge and our machinery have been developed. We have developed new abilities, since those we needed before are not needed now. Such development will be continuous as our economy grows and changes with its growth.

Perhaps the greatest handicap to development of abilities latent in all Americans is the industrialists' lack of understanding and belief in the possibilities of the wage earner. Industry needs developed men. They are the source of industrial progress. Industry's present program for the development of man falls far short of what it should be. It is a program for developing executives and engineers. It almost entirely overlooks the development of the hourly worker, its greatest potential asset.

Today, because of habit, we industrial managers are all too apt to think of the wage earner as merely a member of a union that is trying to ruin the company by high wages and low productivity. Industrial leadership must meet this challenge. Industrial leadership must provide incentives that will inspire the individual wage earner to develop his latent abilities and give him the opportunity to rise as far as these developed abilities can carry him.

If industrial leadership is to develop the worker as it can, the leaders must take an entirely new view of their responsibilities. The wage earner is not a man apart. He has become so only because managers have thought of him that way. They have not thought of him

143

as a fellow player on the same team. This necessary realism is the first step toward making the man the valuable partner that he can be. When management recognizes that the results we all want to accomplish in industry can only be achieved by mutual cooperation, the first step will have been taken toward development of that cooperation and toward the personal development of all the men involved.

Again, we managers must follow the Christian philosophy. The Golden Rule is not solely a religious concept. It is the practical rule for men to follow in their relationships with each other. There is too little realization that only by following this rule can we succeed in all the endeavors of our daily lives. That is why men find so much difficulty in working together. We think of the Christian ethic as something that is for Sunday only. We do not actually believe it to the extent of following its precepts in all our dealings with others.

When men accept each other as Christ taught, we will have an entirely different relationship from what we have now. We will eliminate the friction now common. Mutual understanding and willing cooperation will replace it. Men will develop their abilities to the fullest and devise endless new and better methods and products. The willing cooperation of developed men will make unimaginable progress. The standard of living will rise to heights undreamed of now. We will all be far happier. We need only be practical enough to see that Christ stated a fundamental and necessary principle.

144

12

Conclusion

THE difficulties that we face in operating industry are similar to those faced in any group action. The problem always is, what will be the reaction of those affected by our program? We want to get the cooperation of the customer so he will buy from us rather than from abroad. We also must get the cooperation of the workers from top to bottom in our manufacturing operations to get costs down. We want to get the cooperation of the stockholder so that he will not upset our program. All of these cooperations are essential for continuous success. Lack of support from any of these groups can be a handicap. Complete lack of cooperation will mean the end of the company.

Industry now usually follows a program that is far from successful in encouraging cooperation. This is the result of long established habits and therefore change is hard to come by. We do not earn the goodwill of the customer. We do not deserve it. We let hired "experts" concoct our relations with him and try to delude him about our products. We charge him all we can get out of him. Nothing but competition holds prices down and keeps quality from being worse than it is.

Industrialists try to eliminate competition by patents, tariffs and so-called "fair trade laws." If industry can by patents eliminate competition, that program is gleefully followed. When patents control, the price is kept high and progress is largely neglected. Industry's leaders follow this philosophy, both by act and belief. The customer is exploited in spite of the fact that his continuous buying is completely necessary if industry is to continue to exist.

Industrial leaders also have followed a policy that is far from practical in their contacts with the workers on whom they must depend for progress in reducing costs. A wage-earner very rarely has management to thank for an advance in income or status. He gets such gains from the labor union that compels management to grant them. In spite of the fact that the worker's wages are the buying power that supports industry, the industrial managers do not want to increase them. Many would like to reduce them, which would reduce buying power and if carried far enough would eventually ruin all industry. If wages were now at the level of a generation ago, most industries could never have been started. How many of the products of industry could the wage-earner buy on wages of 20 cents per hour and less, the standard rate fifty years ago?

The present policy of operating industry for the benefit of the stockholder is not a reasonable one. The trouble is that the reward now given to the stockholder is usually far too much and it is given to the wrong person. Because the stockholder owns the company he forces from management large dividends. Management pays these dividends by taking too much from the customer through high prices. The stockholder also gets income that should go to the worker as reward for increased efficiency, since it is only the worker's efficiency that can reduce costs of production and increase profit. The usual absentee stockholder contributes nothing to the efficiency of the operation. He buys a stock today and sells it tomorrow. He often does not even know what the company makes. Why should he be rewarded by large dividends?

It is obvious that the philosophy of much industrial management is far from rational. We see its results in continually higher prices, frequent strikes and increased dividends. These results are becoming ever more disastrous to the economy. Strikes are costing billions of dollars and an even greater loss in terms of possible progress not made. We are falling behind in world competition. We will soon lose our leading place in the family of nations, either to foreign competition, or because of a war for which we are preparing at breakneck speed. The necessity for taking a new look is obvious and urgent.

Let us begin by realizing that man, the individual person, creates all conditions in the human world.

Industrial companies are a part of this world. Man creates them. Industrial production is part of man's activities. His activities come from his nature, the nature of human beings. All our problems, then, begin in the nature of man, and in trying to solve them we must understand the nature of man.

What elements in human nature are relevant to the problems of the men responsible for the existence and future of American industry?

Men inherently strive to outdo others in anything they attempt. To excel is the goal. It is the fundamental urge in everyone. In athletics we want to win or break records others have made. In driving a car we want to pass the car ahead. In science we want to advance further than anyone else. In bestowing kindness we have the same desire. We want to return to others more than we receive.

Man is always in competition with other men. The problem is to make the competition useful so that it will develop men's goals in the proper direction. That is why the Christian ethic is necessary, and why it succeeds if men follow it. That is why the Golden Rule works when it is followed.

It is this basic fact in human nature that makes the

148

philosophy of Christ applicable and practical in our relations with each other.

The Hebrews advanced a step from barbarism when they said that if we hurt another only as much as he hurt us we would balance the account and close it. No further reprisal would be called for. The ethic of "an eye for an eye and a tooth for a tooth" represented progress from the barbarism that then prevailed everywhere in savage antiquity. But further progress and the proper use of the competitive urge in man's nature resulted in "As ye would that others do unto you, do ye even so to them."

This Christian ethic solves every problem that man can have in his association with others. Acting according to it is the way toward a better life. Acting contrary to it is the way to lose everything we value in life.

How does acting according to the Christian ethic solve the problems of industrial management? First, a manager who accepts it will recognize every employee as a fellow human being, whose self-respect, skill and advancement are as important to him as the manager's own are to him. This will change the attitude of managers to the labor force and their reaction to him.

Management now does not think of the hourly worker as an individual with all the problems and human attributes of any man and with unique personal qualities of his own. The wage earner is a fellow worker. Still the manager will not treat him as a human being who has the desires and hopes that the manager has. Instead, he regards the worker as an enemy who is trying to

149

wreck the company by strikes, featherbedding and wage rates that will price the company's product out of the market.

Certainly, the programs that unions have adopted will do just that if managers continue to do as they are now doing. The threat is very obvious and frightening. The reason that it exists is that managers have failed in the leadership that is their responsibility. If managers in the past had been the leaders that employees must have and expect, if they had treated men as men and not as commodities or figures in a ledger, workers would never have found a union boss to lead them.

When strikes occur, management has failed in its function of leadership. There is a long record of such failure to be erased. There is justified resentment and suspicion by the worker to overcome. The task requires absolute sincerity and honesty and inexhaustible patience. Managers must recognize that the men's wariness and suspicion are justified by their past experience.

When we accept the Christian ethic, we in management make the worker's progress a major aim of our policy. Our company must win in a competitive market. To develop a team that can win in such competition we must care for the well-being and development of every man in the plant as an athletic coach looks out for every member of his team. When we do that, an entirely different attitude develops in the worker. He responds as members of a team do, with his full cooperation. If he feels, as he must, that management is trying to help him in his striving for a better life, he will with great enthusiasm repay the management by greater efforts to help accomplish the goals that management has. Such a reaction is automatic in man. It always occurs. Men automatically respond to sincerity with even greater sincerity. That is the reason that the Christian ethic is always successful in practice.

There are many forms and degrees of cooperation between the worker and management. The worker's attitude can vary all the way from passivity to highly imaginative contributions to efficiency and progress. When the first cautious thawing develops into genuine team-spirit, however, the difference that it makes in an industry is the difference between the speed with which the union worker usually approaches his job after a coffee break and the agility with which he plays a game.

Enthusiastic cooperation of men in industry increases efficiency enormously. It multiplies production. It cuts costs. It raises wages, while it constantly lowers prices to the customer.

This difference in the spirit of the men is fundamental, but it is hard to measure or describe. However, it shows itself in the help that the hourly worker gives in developing new ways of production, in saving materials and time. It shows in the continuous operation of machines compared to the breakdowns on these same machines when the workers don't care. Like friendship between two people, the spirit of cooperation is intangible, but its effects are great.

The solving of the difficulties that beset American in-

151

dustry is part of our national problem. A sound, healthy and progressing economy resulting from following the Christian ethic is basic to our country's future. We have the ability to lead the world in production as we have done before, yet we are being outdistanced by foreign competition in many places. This is no doubt caused to an extent by our drift to socialism. Dependence on government for support weakens people and has always led to the decline of the countries that have adopted it. In our own field, however, we industrial managers see that labor-management friction has reduced efficiency and hampered progress. We can also see examples of unhampered and continuing expansion and progress in industries where workers and managers are enthusiastically cooperating. We need only to follow this well-established policy.

New leadership is necessary. American industry must have leaders whom men will follow enthusiastically. Old ways of thinking, old customs and routines must be discarded. In times even more desperate than these, when enemy troops were on our shores and Americans lacked powder for their muskets, a refugee sharpened his quill pen and wrote: "There hath not been such an opportunity since the time of Adam. We have it in our power to make a new world."

Americans have made a world beyond this refugee's power to imagine. Nothing like the bounties of American life has ever before existed on earth. Now we have this new world to protect and preserve and make always newer and better. There has never been a greater opportunity for American industrial leaders. They must rise to it as they always have done.

What are the characters and qualities so greatly needed in an industrial leader?

FIRST: In all his acts and conclusions he will be guided by the philosophy of Christ, given in the Sermon on the Mount and the New Commandment. The outward evidences of sincere acceptance of the Christian philosophy are complete honesty and fairness in thought and acts. These are essential to successful leadership. Man will not follow willingly any other kind of leader. The successful leader must be completely trusted. Therefore, he must be completely trustworthy.

SECOND: The leader must have the knowledge and imagination to determine the direction of the company's progress. His is the responsibility for planning the necessary changes in methods and in products. He must also determine how he will put in the necessary incentive from top to bottom of his organization, in order to continually develop his workers' latent abilities. This development will largely determine the rate of the company's progress.

THIRD: The leader must give a continuous spur to the organization so that it will not become static. Here example and enthusiasm are the basis of success. As progress is made, there is always a great tendency to rest on the oars and stop trying. He must eliminate them in himself as well as in all others in the organization.

FOURTH: The leader must accept a rather cloistered life. He cannot be the extrovert friend to all the people he would like to be with. His decisions must be objective always and in all things. His life is to a considerable extent determined by his job and the necessities that such leadership puts on him. Success on his job must be his goal, to which all other

153

desires, outside of his family, must be secondary. He will be well rewarded financially. His greatest reward, however, will be the feeling of accomplishment. If that is not a sufficient incentive, it would be well for him to look elsewhere for a satisfactory life. All great accomplishments are apt to segregate the person who makes the progress. Success always has set its people apart.

Appendix

Some Actual Results

THE fundamental philosophy of a successful manufacturing program has been outlined in the
twelve preceding chapters. Some of the results that have
actually been obtained are shown in this Appendix.

The following charts do not accurately show the
relative production of the incentive program compared
to that made by the usual manufacturer, since the price
of the product made under the incentive system was
reduced during the period shown while the prices of
the products made under the other system were greatly
increased. The comparison is far from an accurate
showing of the relative efficiencies of production under the two systems.

What is produced by the worker is pieces of product, not dollars. To compare the relative productivity,
the pieces produced should be shown. That is not possi-

ble, since the products are different. Dollars of value is the only way that production can be measured, since there is no other common denominator.

Since production can only be measured in dollars, the rise in price of the products shown, made by the usual methods, means that the number of parts produced is less than one-third of what is shown if the price were constant. The products made under the incentive system have remained nearly constant in price. In fact, the prices have gone down.

For a proper comparison, therefore, the production under the incentive plan must be increased by at least three times, or the products made by the usual methods must be reduced to one-third of that shown. In either case, the productivity of the incentive-made products is more than six times that of the usually produced products, not twice, as shown by the chart.

It will be startling, perhaps to see this difference. The result is not unusual. All incentive systems that have achieved cooperation between so-called labor and management have had similar experiences. A very good illustration was the result that Henry Ford the first achieved. He reduced the cost and price of the Model T Ford from $950 to $290 in twenty years with no change in the car. He paid twice the going wage rate and made a fortune for the owners by his program.

Such results are automatic when the proper philosophy is adopted which results in cooperation between labor and management. While the results are surprising to those who have not had experience with them, they are usual. They are like the relative speeds of an athlete breaking a record or walking in his sleep.

CHART I

Since 1934, the year that our incentive program was started, costs have increased substantially.

Labor, copper and steel sheets and bars are major cost elements in a motor-generator welder. Yet in spite of these increases, the selling price now is approximately 20 per cent less than it was in 1934.

WELDER SELLING PRICE IN RELATION TO COSTS
300 AMPERE MOTOR-GENERATOR
(See footnotes page 158)

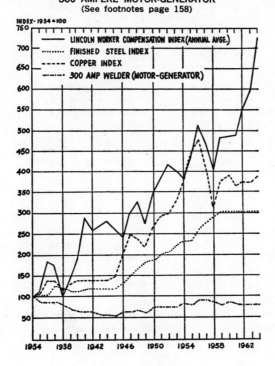

157

TABLE • *Indexes of Lincoln Worker Compensation, cost of Finished Steel and Copper, and selling price of 300 Amp Welders, 1934–1965.* (1934 = 100)

	Worker Compensation[a]	Finished Steel[b]	Copper[b]	300 Amp Welder[a]
1934	100.0	100.0	100.0	100.0
1935	111.6	100.8	106.3	88.4
1936	179.7	103.3	134.8	88.4
1937	170.7	123.6	134.8	88.4
1938	99.2	119.9	116.0	80.6
1939	142.7	112.7	126.8	71.3
1940	193.7	112.2	133.7	67.4
1941	294.8	116.8	134.8	64.3
1942	259.5	116.8	134.8	64.3
1943	273.3	116.8	134.8	58.9
1944	285.0	116.8	134.8	55.8
1945	264.7	119.4	148.0	55.8
1946	244.8	131.0	198.4	62.8
1947	298.7	146.9	248.0	62.8
1948	331.4	167.4	237.9	67.4
1949	283.9	181.0	222.0	65.9
1950	352.0	188.3	261.7	76.7
1951	383.8	201.4	277.7	76.7
1952	419.6	206.6	301.4	76.7
1953	404.8	220.3	333.1	76.7
1954	388.6	229.9	380.7	78.4
1955	439.4	242.7	444.1	78.4
1956	512.3	261.2	475.9	92.2
1957	464.5	282.8	411.4	92.2
1958	404.4	295.5	331.4	88.4
1959	478.4	302.1	377.1	83.7
1960	485.8	302.1	393.3	86.8
1961	489.0	302.1	371.4	82.9
1962	547.4	302.1	377.3	82.9
1963	594.4	303.9[b]	377.3	82.9
1964	715.3	306.0[b]	392.6	82.9

[a] Computed from Company records.
[b] The steel and copper indexes are based on price series carried in *Iron Age, American Metal Market* and *Steel* magazines.

158

The machine is essentially the same, with of course improvements and refinements. The profit per dollar of sales has remained approximately constant during the period shown.

CHART II

The price of steel rod, the raw material from which welding electrodes are cut and drawn, has increased substantially since 1934. The selling price of 5/32-inch Fleetweld 5 electrode is less now than it was in 1934.

ELECTRODE SELLING PRICE IN RELATION TO COST OF STEEL ROD

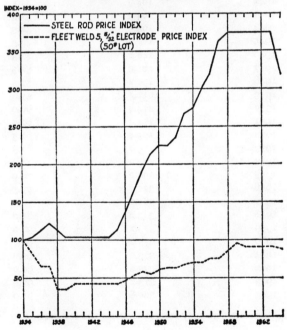

159

Welding electrode is a steel rod drawn to a relatively small diameter and covered with a complex chemical coating.

T A B L E • *Price Indexes of rod and FW 5 Electrodes.*[a] (1934 = 100)

	Steel Rod Price	FW 5 Electrodes
1934	100.0	100.0
1935	104.9	82.5
1936	112.2	65.0
1937	121.9	65.0
1938	112.2	37.5
1939	104.9	37.5
1940	104.9	42.5
1941	104.9	42.5
1942	104.9	42.5
1943	104.9	42.5
1944	104.9	42.5
1945	112.2	42.5
1946	148.8	47.5
1947	161.0	52.5
1948	190.2	57.5
1949	212.2	55.0
1950	224.4	60.0
1951	224.4	62.5
1952	235.4	62.5
1953	265.8	67.5
1954	273.2	70.0
1955	300.0	70.0
1956	320.7	77.5
1957	361.0	77.5
1958	373.2	85.0
1959	373.2	90.0
1960	373.2	90.0
1961	373.2	90.0
1962	373.2	90.0
1963	373.2	90.0
1964	320.8	85.0

[a] Computed from Company records of prices and rod costs.

These results as shown have been developed because of new machinery for production, better use of materials, better design, as well as greater skill of the operator. This advance was made possible because of the cooperation and development of the latent abilities of the people involved. The profit margin per dollar of sales remained approximately constant during the period shown.

CHART III

The productivity of the Lincoln organization as measured by sales value of product per employee is more than double that of the average of all manufacturing industries in the United States as classified and determined by the U. S. Department of Commerce Statistics. The sales value of products per employee shown is determined by dividing the total number of Lincoln Electric employees, including all branch sales and warehouse personnel, into the total dollar volume for the year.

SALES VALUE OF PRODUCTS PER EMPLOYEE

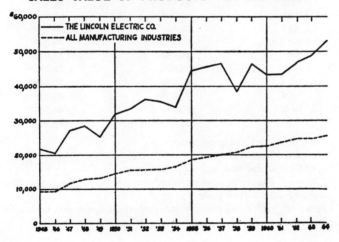

161

Had the sales value been shown in units instead of dollars, the difference would have been more than six to one, instead of two to one, as shown. What is produced by the worker is obviously finished products, not dollars. It is not possible to show the comparison of production in any other way than in dollars, however.

TABLE • *Showing Productivity Per Worker, Measured by Sales Dollar, for The Lincoln Electric Company, and All Manufacturers.*

Year	The Lincoln Electric Co.[a]	All Manufacturers[b]
1945	$21,897	$ 9,135
1946	20,323	9,446
1947	27,050	11,684
1948	28,354	12,896[y]
1949	25,012	13,007
1950	31,736	14,484
1951	33,116	15,583
1952	35,677	15,640
1953	35,113	15,832
1954	33,892	16,572
1955	44,142	18,280
1956	45,738	19,098
1957	46,495	20,002
1958	38,169	20,348[z]
1959	46,152	22,075[z]
1960	43,068	22,296[z]
1961	43,074	23,220[z]
1962	46,936	23,717[z]
1963	49,011	24,539[z]
1964	53,869	25,794[z]

[a] Computed from Company records.
[b] Computed from *National Income*, various years, Supplement to *Survey of Current Business*, U.S. Dept. of Commerce.
[y] Change in base from 1948 on introduces a slight degree of non-comparability with earlier years.
[z] Series originally used now discontinued, these values estimated from other series.

CHART IV

The average hourly earnings of production workers and non-supervisory manufacturing personnel of The Lincoln Electric Company are more than double those of production workers in industries classified by the Bureau of Labor in the category of All Manufacturing Industries.

AVERAGE HOURLY EARNINGS OF PRODUCTION WORKERS

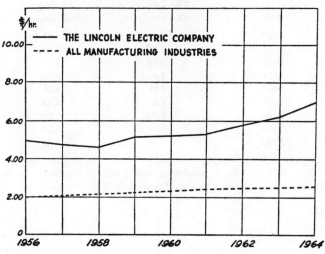

Although the average hourly earnings of Lincoln production workers greatly exceed those paid by other companies, when it is converted to labor cost per unit for the same production, the labor cost per unit is much lower than that of the other companies. This lower cost of labor is given to the

163

A NEW APPROACH TO INDUSTRIAL ECONOMICS

customer in lower prices, as is shown in the preceding charts.
It is a company program not only to reward the producer for
what he does but also most importantly to reward the customer by lower prices.

TABLE • *Average Hourly Earnings of production workers and non-
supervisory manufacturing personnel of The Lincoln Electric Company
and All Manufacturing Industries. Earnings include overtime pre-
miums, bonus, retirement annuities, vacation pay and other fringe
benefits. The earnings of management, engineering, sales and office
personnel have been excluded from these figures—1956–1964*

Year	The Lincoln Electric Co.[a]	All Mfg. Industries[b]
1956	$4.90	$1.95
1957	4.76	2.05
1958	4.60	2.11
1959	5.14	2.19
1960	5.20	2.26
1961	5.29	2.32
1962	5.82	2.39
1963	6.22	2.46
1964	6.99	2.54

[a] Computed from Company records.
[b] Obtained from the Employment and Earnings Statistics for the
United States, Bureau of Labor Statistics Bulletin #1312–2.

CHART V

There are no layoffs at The Lincoln Electric Company when business slumps. Employment is continuous. There is only retirement at advanced age and the occasional drop-off when the man does not fit.

Few workers will leave the job that is a source of recognized benefit and great development of latent abilities. Development of latent abilities cannot be shown in detail but is one of the reasons for the enormous progress that is shown in cost reduction.

MONTHLY LABOR TURNOVER RATE

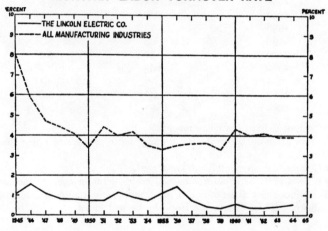

165

TABLE • *Stability of Work Force as Measured by Monthly Labor Separation Rate for Lincoln Electric and U.S. Industry 1945–1964*

	Lincoln Electric[a]	All Industry[b]
1945	1.07	8.0
1946	1.60	5.9
1947	1.10	4.7
1948	.81	4.4
1949	.79	4.1
1950	.73	3.4
1951	.75	4.4
1952	1.17	4.0
1953	.90	4.2
1954	.73	3.5[x]
1955	1.11	3.3[x]
1956	1.44	3.5[x]
1957	.72	3.6
1958	.43	3.6
1959	.33	3.3[x]
1960	.51	3.3[x]
1961	.32	4.0[z]
1962	.36	4.1[z]
1963	.42	3.9[z]
1964	.51	3.9[z]

[a] Computed from Company records.
[b] From *Monthly Labor Review,* various dates, Bureau of Labor Statistics data.
[x] Computed from monthly rates averaged.
[z] Bureau of Labor Statistics revised entire index in 1960 to include Food Processing Industries and the printing, publishing, and related industries. These figures are from the revised index.